THE RHYTHM BOOK

2nd edition

RICHARD HOFFMAN
Belmont University

Franklin, Tennessee, USA

2009

www.takadimi.net

for Benjamin and Caleb

The Rhythm Book, 2nd edition

Published by Harpeth River Publishing
2048 Belmont Circle, Franklin, Tenn. 37069

Printed in Nashville, Tennessee
The United States of America

Printing number: 7 6 5 4 3

ISBN-13: 978-098372870-2

✧ CONTENTS

✧ On studying rhythm — Notes for students and teachers

Music is sometimes defined as "sound organized in time." A large part of the temporal or "time" element of music is what we commonly call rhythm. I should be clear from the beginning that what we are really studying is for the most part "Western tonal rhythm" the rhythm that developed along with Western tonal music. Western tonal music refers to music derived from the art music and to some extent the folk music of western Europe over the last 400 years or so. Tonality, the organization around a focal pitch we call "tonic," is the most distinctive feature of this music. It is so pervasive in European-American culture that we often take it for granted. The rhythm of tonal music is also distinctive, and very different from the rhythm of music that is not tonal or music from other parts of the world. How these musical traditions are different is not terribly important right now, but we should acknowledge that the kind of rhythm we are studying is the kind found in Western tonal music.

Using this book will help you learn to read and understand tonal rhythm, and perform it accurately and confidently. Don't rush too quickly through the early, seemingly easy exercises. From the outset work carefully to build good habits, to master the conducting beat patterns, and to learn to pay attention to tempo, dynamics, and articulation markings. It is fine to perform the exercises in ways other than those specified—with other tempos or articulations—but they should never be done in a thoughtless and unmusical way.

Always perform musically. Listen for the phrases and gestures that move the music along. The idea that music has a sense of forward motion is very much a characteristic of tonal music. Don't neglect the motion just because you are working primarily with rhythm. If an exercise begins with a pick-up, subsequent phrases are likely also to begin with a pick-up. Breathe at the phrases breaks (notated or not) and not after the first note of two of the new phrase. Never perform the exercises in a boring monotone. Use your voice to show the direction of the line, the high and low points, and cadences.

There are six types of exercises in the book.

Single parts These exercises are the most common, and are usually designed to address specific issues or introduce new material. Even on a simple, single-line exercise, always perform musically, interpreting the phrases and gestures in a way that shows you understand the musical structure.

Ensembles (duets and trios) These are intended for more than one performer. Always learn all the parts, and switch parts often in performance.

Speak and clap These are intended for a single performer to speak one part and clap the other. Typically you should speak the top line and clap the lower, but occasionally switching parts is good practice.

Layering These exercises combine repeated patterns or ostinatos in various ways. You can repeat each pattern an agreed upon number of times, or allow the performers to determine how and how often the parts are to be repeated. Occasionally ostinatos are provided for other single line exercises. You may layer these in a variety of creative ways as well. Layering patterns and ostinato rhythms in this way is more akin to certain African and East Asian styles of music.

Improvise in the blanks These exercises have blank measures in which you should improvise rhythm. Try to use rhythms that relate to the exercise. Always pay attention to the music that comes before and after, and make sure your improvised material fits.

Real music These exercises are written on a staff to give practice reading rhythm in a more familiar musical setting. Although these are still primarily rhythm exercises, use the cues of contour and phrasing to give a musical performance.

In addition to the rhythm exercises, there are both pre-notational and written exercises. Do these exercises as they occur, and use them as models to create your own supplemental exercise.

Other suggestions for practice

Echo rhythm. Speak or clap rhythms to a study partner, and have the partner respond on Ta'kadimi syllables. This is a very effective way to learn rhythm, and should come before reading and writing with notation.

Experiment. Include the element of pitch. Singing rhythm on one repeated pitch puts strain on your voice and is not recommended. But singing on a scale or even improvising a melody is great practice and strongly encouraged. When singing scales sometimes it is easier and more sensible to change pitches with each beat or even each measure.

Be creative. Use the exercises in the book as a basis for creating your own exercises. For example you might add ostinatos or improvised clapping parts where none is given, or consider the given exercise the first phrase of a two phrase period, and improvise a subsequent phrase. There are many ways to expand on the framework given in the text. Through play is a natural way to learn new skills. Think of all you learned as a child just by playing. Find creative ways to "play" with rhythm. It will make learning fun and effective.

Multi-task. It is fine to work just on the rhythm when learning a new concept or working out a challenging pattern, but it is important to add other elements to your performance as you become more proficient. Once you have overcome the technical challenges of an exercise, always conduct, clap, sing pitches, or do something else to expand your performance. Rarely in real music do we focus solely on rhythm. Even in percussion music, performers are thinking about timbre, style, and musical expression, even when playing a single rhythmic line.

Special thanks

Special thanks are owed to Nashville composer and percussionist David Madeira. David worked with me especially on the later chapters in the book to write examples that were challenging and reflecting current musical trends.

Takadimi

Takadimi is the system of rhythmic solfege used throughout the book. It does for rhythm what "*do re mi*" solfege does for pitch. It gives us a way to label the parts of a rhythm and can make it easier both to understand and to perform. Takadimi is beat oriented; that is, it assigns syllables based on the position of the note within the beat. It is also pattern based. Reading rhythm with Takadimi helps you learn to recognize rhythmic patterns and see groupings of notes, not simply read note to note. Reading rhythm this way is similar to the way we read groups of letters as words and not one letter at a time. The word "takadimi" is similar to a pattern used in the complex system of chanted sounds used to learn Indian drumming. Indian music is not metric in the way tonal rhythm is, and so its use in that system is entirely different from the way we use it here.

The Takadimi system as described in this book was developed in the early 1990s by several members of the theory faculty at Ithaca College in Ithaca, New York. The article that introduced the system was co-authored by Richard Hoffman, William Pelto, and John W. White, and titled "Takadimi: A Beat-Oriented system of Rhythmic Solfege," and published in the *Journal of Music Theory Pedagogy* (1994). The article thoroughly explains the system and shows its relation to other similar system of learning rhythm.

I must thank my co-authors, Bill Pelto and John White, as well as the others who worked with us from the early stages of Takadimi, especially: John Benoit, Craig Cummings, and Timothy Nord. I must also thank the many teachers in schools across the country who have successfully used Takadimi, and in so doing have continued to add to its pedagogical value. Thanks are owed my colleagues at Belmont University who have used Takadimi and this book, especially Kris Elsberry, Deen Entsminger, Todd Kemp, Brent Gerlach, David Madeira, Caleb Weeks, and Margie Yankeelov. Their insight and skillful application in the classroom have been both an inspiration and a very practical help. Finally, I must thank the many students who have learned rhythm with Takadimi and showed us what worked and what didn't, and most of all, inspired us to keep trying.

1 ✧ Getting started with rhythm and meter

Pulse and beat

Most Western tonal music, which includes most classical music and virtually all American popular and folk music, maintains a sense of steady ***pulse***. This is why you can clap to it, dance to it, or march to it. It is also why we can have a sense of speeding up or slowing down. Not all music works this way, but most does, and that is where our study begins. The easiest way to understand pulse is to experience it. Sing any familiar song and clap along at a steady rate. You are clapping a pulse. I say *a* pulse because actually there are many levels of pulse in most music. Try clapping a pulse that is faster or slower than the one you started with. Each represents a different level of pulse.

The ***beat*** is one specific level of the pulse. Usually what we feel as "the beat" falls within the range of about 60 – 180 beats per minute, roughly within the range of the human heart beat. Musicians might sometimes disagree about which level of the pulse is *the beat*, and sometimes there is no one right answer.

Meter

Meter is the grouping of beats into patterns of strong and weak accents. In the analysis of meter, a dash indicates a strong beat and a curved line indicates a weak beat, like this:

— ∪ — ∪
strong weak strong weak

There are three common metric groupings:

duple meter (2 beats) — ∪

triple meter (3 beats) — ∪ ∪

quadruple meter (4 beats) — ∪ – ∪

Duple meter groups two beats together in the pattern: "accented — unaccented" or "strong — weak." Speak this pattern and clap on the word "strong." The song "Three Blind Mice" is in duple meter. Sing the song and clap on the accented beat.

– ∪ – ∪ – ∪ – ∪ – ∪ – ∪ – ∪ – ∪
Three blind mice, Three blind mice, see how they run, see how they run . . . etc.

Triple meter groups three beats together in the pattern. "My Country 'Tis of Thee" is in triple meter. Sing and clap the accented beats.

– ∪ ∪ – ∪ ∪ – ∪ ∪ – ∪ ∪ – ∪ ∪ – ∪ ∪
My coun-try 'tis of thee, Sweet land of li- ber-ty. Of thee I sing . . . etc.

Quadruple meter groups four beats together in the pattern. In this meter the third beat is somewhat accented, but not as strongly accented as the first beat. Quadruple meter may also be thought of as a variant of two groups of duple meter.

— ∪ – ∪ — ∪ – ∪ — ∪ – ∪ — ∪ – ∪
Are you sleep-ing, Are you sleep-ing Broth - er John, Broth - er John etc.

Measure

A *measure* shows the accent groups. There are six measures in the example below. Each repetition of the pattern marks a new measure.

| – ∪ ∪ | – ∪ ∪ | – ∪ ∪ | – ∪ ∪ | – ∪ ∪ | – ∪ ∪ |
My coun-try 'tis of thee, Sweet land of li- ber- ty. Of thee I sing . . . etc.

Division of the beat

Meter can be classified by how the beat note is divided.

Simple meter: A meter with a beat note that divides into two smaller notes is called a *simple meter.*

Sing "Camptown Races." Notice that each beat can be divided into two smaller pulses.

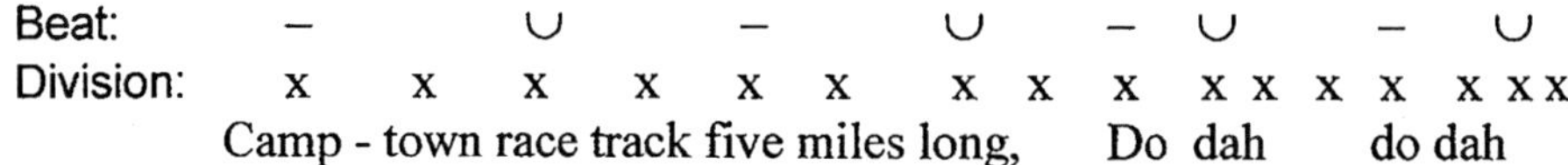

Compound meter: A meter with a beat note that divides into three is called a *compound meter.*

Sing "Over the River and Through the Woods." Notice that the beat can be divided into three smaller pulses.

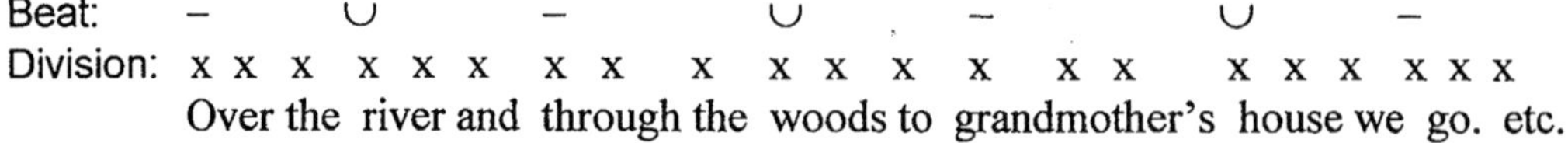

Classifying Meter

Any meter can be classified based on these two criteria:

→ the number of beats in a measure: duple, triple, quadruple

→ how the beat is divided: simple or compound

Meter signature

A meter signature (or time signature) consists of two numbers placed one above the other, and usually located at the beginning of a piece of music. It tells us how the piece is organized metrically. The lower number tells us a note value, and the top number tells us how many notes of that value fit in a measure.

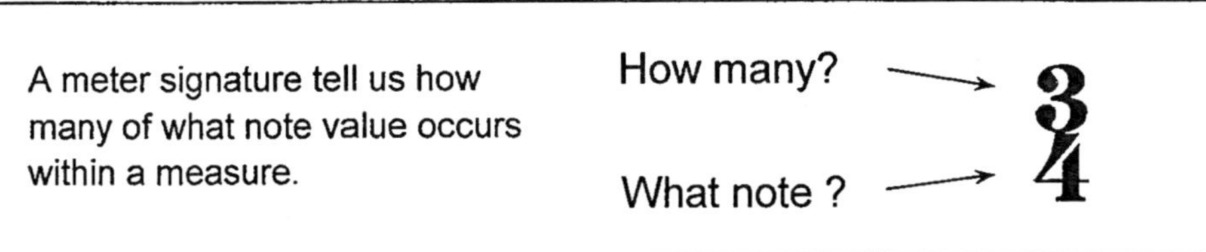

Caution! The meter signature *doesn't* always tell us how many *beats* are in the measure, so let's take this one step at a time.

Meters signatures have slightly different meanings depending on whether they occur in simple or compound meter. In a simple meter (a meter in which the beat note divides in two parts) the bottom number tells us the value of the beat note. But in compound meter (a meter in which the beat divides in three parts) the bottom number tells us the value of the ***division*** of the beat.

Simple Meter		**Compound Meter**	
How many?	4	How many?	6
Value of beat note?	4	Value of beat division?	8

By regrouping the divisions, we can tell how many beats are in the measure of compound meter. (***Note:*** A dot adds one half the value of a note. So in the example below, two eighth notes equals a quarter note, and the dot adds half the value of a quarter note, that is another eighth note.)

Compound meters always have 6, 9, or 12 as the top number of the meter signature. You can always tell how many beats are in the measure by dividing (grouping) by three.

The reason behind this difference in terminology is fairly easy to understand. Most rhythmic values can be easily represented by a number. To represent a quarter note by a 4 or a half note by a 2, for example, is sensible and intuitive. But the beat note in compound meters is always a dotted note, and dotted notes are not easy to represent with whole numbers. A compound meter signature, therefore, shows the number of *divisions* of the beat and the value of the division, something that can always be expressed in whole numbers.

Below are some common meter signatures showing the type of meter and the beat note.

Beat note	𝅝	𝅗𝅥	♩	♪
Simple duple	2/1	2/2	2/4	2/8
Simple triple	3/1	3/2	3/4	3/8
Simple quadruple	4/1	4/2	4/4	4/8

Beat note	𝅝.	𝅗𝅥.	♩.	♪.
Compound duple	6/2	6/4	6/8	6/16
Compound triple	9/2	9/4	9/8	9/16
Compound quadruple	12/2	12/4	12/8	12/16

Alternative meter signatures

In the middle of the 20th century, a number of composers and publishers experimented with a method of showing meter signatures using actual notes instead of numbers for the bottom number of the meter signature.

4 over ♩ = $\frac{4}{4}$ 2 over ♩. = $\frac{6}{8}$ 3 over 𝅗𝅥. = ?

This method has the advantage of being consistent and intuitive, but unfortunately it never caught on.

Conducting

Conducting the beat is a good way to learn to experience meter. Conducting patterns are designed so that strong beats always have a motion downward.

Basic Conducting Patterns:

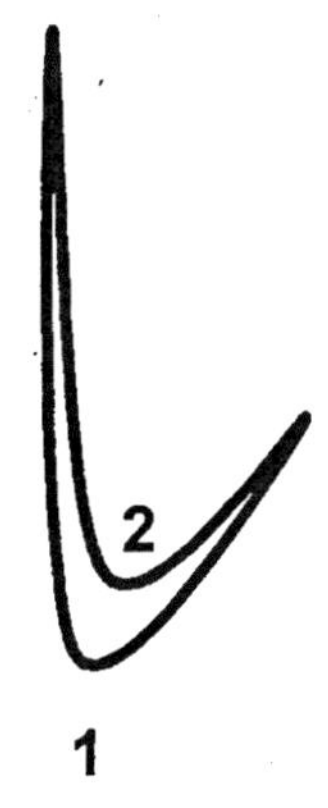

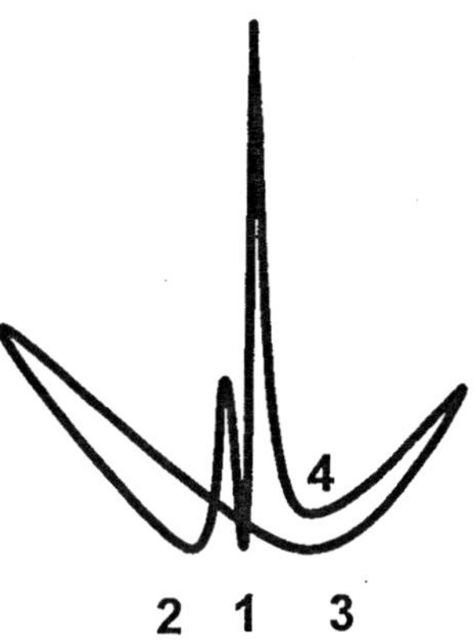

Conducting Tips:

- Always feel a bounce on the beat, almost as though the heal of your hand is rebounding off of a little trampoline. Don't slide through the bottom of the beats. Your performers need to know exactly where the beat occurs.
- Keep your arm up, elbow away from your body, and move freely from the shoulder. Don't flap your wrist!
- Keep the bottom of your beats centered and even with the middle of your torso. This way the performers can see your face and your conducting pattern at the same time.

Tempo

Tempo tells us how fast or slowly the beat occurs. Tempo indications can be very specific when expressed as beats per minute. A metronome, for example, counts beats per minute. The marking "M.M. = 72" indicates 72 beats per minute. (M.M. stands for "Maelzel Metronome" named for Johann Nepomuk Maelzel, the Austrian inventor who invented a type of mechanical metronome around 1815).

There are a number of foreign terms used to indicate tempo. The most familiar are from Italian. Although the terms do not indicate a specific number of beats per minute, it is worth remembering the general meaning and the relationships among the common terms.

Largo	Lento	Adagio	Andante	Moderato	Allegro	Vivace	Presto
very slow	slow	slow	walking pace	moderate	fast	quick	very fast

Our perception of tempo seems to be tied with our natural body rhythms like breathing, heart rate, or walking. If the beat is faster than our heart rate, for example, it feels relatively fast. In the same way, when the beat is slower than we can comfortably walk, it feels very slow.

2 ✧ Simple meter

Simple meters have beat notes that can be divided into two divisions. Here are some familiar songs in simple meter. Clap the beat, then clap the division. What other familiar songs can you name?

Jingle Bells   Auld Lang Syne   My Country 'Tis of Thee   Yankee Doodle

Takadimi (see preface for more on the history of the system)

Takadimi is a system of syllables used for speaking rhythm. The system is beat oriented. In other words, the beat is always spoken on *ta* regardless of the note value. Remember that the beat is just one level of the pulse. The next faster level of the pulse is called the *first division* of the beat (or sometimes called simply *the division* of the beat). A note on the first division of the beat is always called *di*.

Echo-rhythm: With your study partner or instructor, speak or clap and speak back short rhythms using *ta* and *ta di* rhythms. Speak musically and expressively.

> ***Performance tips***
>
> - *Always speak rhythm exercises expressively. Even when phrase marking or dynamics aren't given, perform the rhythm musically.*
> - *Always conduct or keep the beat in a way assigned by your instructor.*

Conduct the appropriate pattern as you perform the following rhythms.

2.1

2.2 Some exercises will include tempo markings. Perform these exercise in the way indicated. Look up any terms you don't know in the appendix.

Moderato

2.3 *Allegro*

2.4 This is a two part exercise. As you perform it with a partner or in class, listen for the *composite rhythm*, that is, the rhythm produced by combining the two parts.

2.5 *Andante*

2.6 The following three exercises are in triple meter.

2.7 ***Flowing***

2.8 ***Moderato***

2.9 The next three exercises are in quadruple meter.

2.10 ***Quickly***

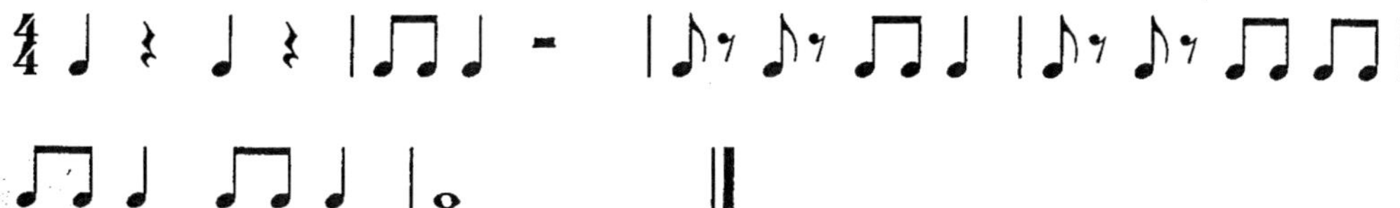

2.11 ***Dolce***

Other beat notes (simple meter)

Any note value can be the beat note, but the beat is always *ta* and the first division always *di*.

2.12

ta ta ta di ta ta di ta di ...

2.13

2.14

2.15 Write these rhythms in the meters indicated. There might be more than one right answer. Perform what you have written.

1. ta ta | ta di ta di | ta ta di | ta

2. ta ta ta di | ta ta di ta di | ta di ta ta | ta

3. ta ta ta di ta | ta di ta di ta ta | ta ta di ta ta di | ta

2.16 *Adagio*

2.17 In two-part rhythms always listen for the *composite rhythm* formed from the interaction of the two parts.

2.18 The note in the last measure is called a "breve" or "double whole note." It is equal in value to two whole notes.

2.19 *Andante*

2.20 ***Largo e legato***

mf *p* *mp* *mf* *f*

2.21 ***Allegretto***

mf *mp*

2.22 ***Presto***

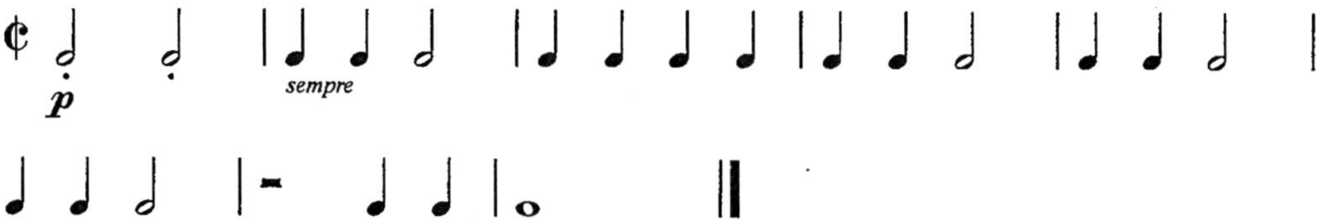

p *sempre*

2.23 ***Allegro***

f

2.24 *Allegro*

The next three exercise are "speak and clap" exercises where one performer performs both parts. Speak one part, usually the upper line, and clap or tap the other. Practice till you can perform them comfortably. "Speak and claps" are always written in this way with one meter signature. Compare the notation to the duet above. This will help you tell them apart.

2.25

2.26

2.27

3 ✧ Pick-up notes

Pick-up notes occur when the phrase begins on a beat other than the strong first beat of the measure. The strong beat or down beat is sometimes called the *crusis*. Pick-up notes or upbeats are then called the *anacrusis*. (*Ana-* is a prefix meaning up or back.) Often subsequent phrases or sub-phrases will also begin on an anacrusis. Be aware of this tendency in the following exercises. Sometimes it is made clear with phrase markings or with rests, but sometimes it is not.

3.1

After you have learned the exercise and are comfortable beginning on the up-beat, clap or speak one or more of the following ostinatos to accompany the exercise. Start the ostinato, then begin the exercise on the correct beat. (An ostinato is a repeated pattern.)

The following exercise includes phrase marking or slurs. Sometimes slurs show actual phrases, but often they simply show notes that should be thought of and performed connected as a group.

3.2 ***Moderato***

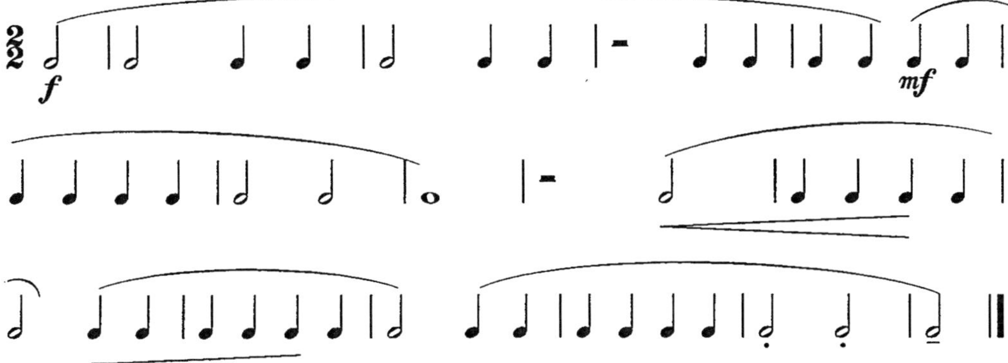

3.3 ***Allegro***

3.4 Set the following texts to rhythm in simple meter. Use only the beat and first division. Include measure lines and a meter signature. Be sure to match the accents in the text with the accents in the meter.

A. "An apple a day keeps the doctor away." *(American proverb)*

B. "Without a shepherd, sheep are not a flock." *(Russian proverb)*

C. "You can't make an omelet without breaking eggs." *(French proverb)*

D. "Whoever really loves you will make you cry." *(Spanish proverb)*

3.5 ***Well marked***

3.6 The "C-slash" meter signature is often called "cut time." Literally it means "alla breve" or "at the half note." It is usually equivalent to 2/2, but can be used to indicate any meter with the half note as the beat note. Be sure to count—and feel!—the exercise in two and not in four. Walk or sway to the beat (in 2) if it helps you feel the meter.

3.7 Learn the following rhythm well, then speak or clap one or more of the following ostinatos to accompany the exercise. Establish the ostinato first, then begin on the correct beat.

3.8 *Presto*

3.9

3.10 *With movement*

3.11 Canon. Listen to the other parts and interact with them musically.

3.12 Speak and clap.

3.13 *Andante*

3.14 Improvise rhythm in the blank measures. Be sure to connect it metrically and rhythmically with what has come before.

3.15 As above, improvise in the blank measures. Make your improvisation fit musically with what has come before.

4 ✧ Second division of the beat

The first division of the beat can be divided again by still shorter pulses. This next level is called the *second division* (or *subdivision*) of the beat. Sing a familiar melody in simple meter. Clap on the beat, then the division, then the second division. Have parts of the class clap each level simultaneously. (Dividing the second division produces the *third division*, and so on.)

Here are the syllables for the beat, first, and second division. Three possible beat notes are shown. Others are possible.

There are six new patterns created using the second division (shown below with the quarter note as the beat). Think carefully about how each is constructed and how it relates to the basic "ta-ka-di-mi" pattern. Think too how each would be written with other beat notes.

Echo-rhythm: With your study partner or instructor, speak or clap and speak back on syllables examples using the beat, division, and second division patterns.

The following six exercises introduce the second division patterns (quarter note = beat note) in context. Practice these exercises at a variety of tempi and dynamic levels. Conduct, clap the beat, or step to the beat while practicing.

4.1

4.2

4.3

4.4

4.5

4.6

4.7 Write these rhythms in the meters indicated. There may be more than one correct solution.

1. ta ta di | ta ka di mi ta di | ta di mi ta di | ta

2/4 | | | ||

2/2 | | | ||

2. ta ta ta di | ta mi ta di ta | ta ta di ta ka di mi| ta

3/4 | | | ||

3/16 | | | ||

3. ta ta di ta di mi ta | ta mi ta di ta ka di ta | ta ta ta ka di mi ta | ta

4/4 | | | ||

4/8 | | | ||

4.8

ta ta ta di ta di ta di ta ka di mi ta di ta di . . .

4.9 *Marcato*

mp

4.10 Rewrite the last four measures of exercise 4.9 in the meter indicated. Write the rhythm syllables beneath the staff.

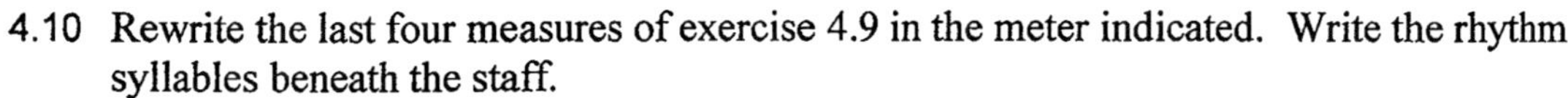

4.11 *Sempre staccato*

4.12 Layer exercise — Assign performers to each of the three parts. You may decide in advance when each line enters and how many times to repeat each section, or each part may move on (or back) independently. The rhythm created by combining two or more parts is called a "composite rhythm." Listen for the composite rhythm produced by the interacting parts. You may also wish to experiment with different timbres, or adding other improvised parts. You may speak, clap or perform on percussion instruments. What things around you might you use in place of instruments?

4.13 *Andante*

4.14

mf *mp*

mf

4.15

4.16 Learn the exercise, then clap or tap one of the ostinatos below as you perform.

ostinatos

4.17 *Moderato* (with improvisation measures)

4.18 *Allegro*

4.19 Write the composite rhythm between the staves. Listen for this composite as you perform the rhythm.

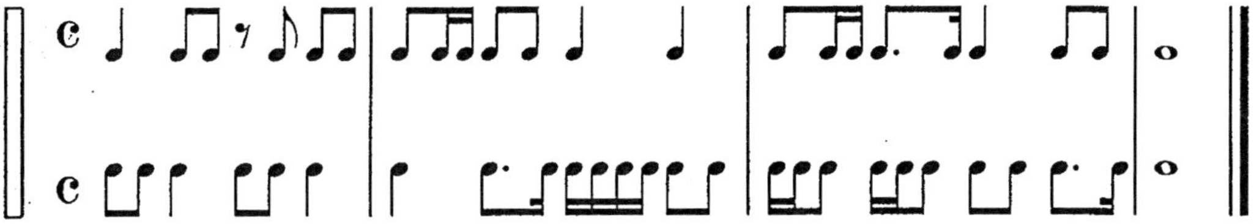

4.20 *Allegro vivo*

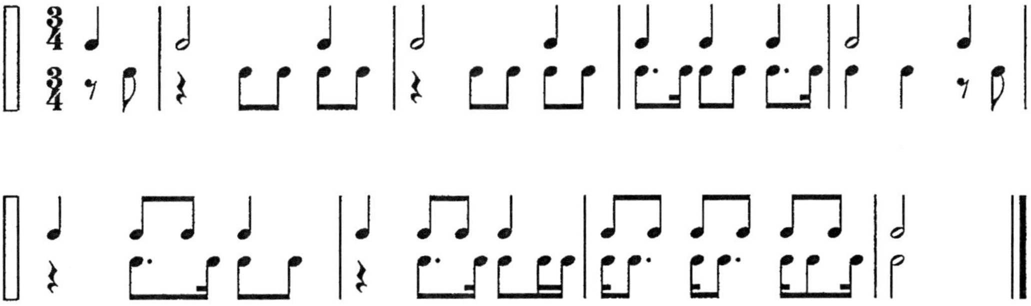

4.21 ***Scherzando***

mf

4.22 ***Animato***

4.23 ***Vigorously***

4.24 ***Flowing*** (with improvisation measures)

mf

4.25 *Allegro*

mf *mp* *mp* *mf* *f* *f*

4.26 *Andante*

4.27 ***Leggiero***

4.28 Layer exercise — You may decide in advance when each line enters and how many times to repeat each section, or each part can move on (or back) independently, or at the direction of a leader. Listen for the composite produced by the interacting parts.

4.29 Duet with improvisation measures

The following examples are written with pitches notated on a standard 5-line staff. Although they are intended as rhythmic exercises, use the cues of contour, grouping, and expression marks to give a musical reading.

5 ✧ Dots and ties

Dots and ties are used in similar ways to extend the duration of a single note value. A dot adds half the value of the non-dotted note. A tie adds the values of the tied notes together as though they were written as one single note. Sometimes either a tie or a dot could be used to create the same duration. The choice of which is best is based on the musical context or the standards of notation.

We have already encountered the dot within the beat (e.g. the *ta – mi* pattern). New to this chapter are dotted or tied beat notes that extend the note beyond the next beat. It is important to "feel" or be aware of the beat covered by the dot or tie. As you practice, first speak the rhythm without the dot. Then replace the dot, still imagining where the missing syllable (in parentheses) should sound. Your teacher may ask you to make a light accent with your voice, or clap on the beat to show exactly where the beat occurs.

5.4 *Allegretto*

5.5 *Adagio*

5.6 *Marcato*

5.7 ***Gentle waltz***

mf

mp

simile

5.8 ***Lively***

5.9 ***Lively***

5.10 ***Con brio*** (with improvisation measures)

5.11 The next three exercises use ties. Some of these could also be written without the ties. How can you decide which to use?

5.12

ta ta ta di (ta) ta ta di ta mi ta . . .

5.13

5.14 Be sure to distinguish between ties and slurs.

5.15 *Allegro* (with improvisation measures)

5.16 Notice that the layers don't all repeat at the same time. Listen for the changing composite rhythm.

I

II

III

5.17

mf

mf

poco rit.

poco rit.

5.18 ***Leggiero***

5.19 Transcribe the first 6 measures of ex 5.18 in the meter indicated. Write the syllables below the notes.

¢

5.20 Canon. Decide before you begin how many times you will repeat the exercise. Once your performance is secure, you might try adding an ostinato.

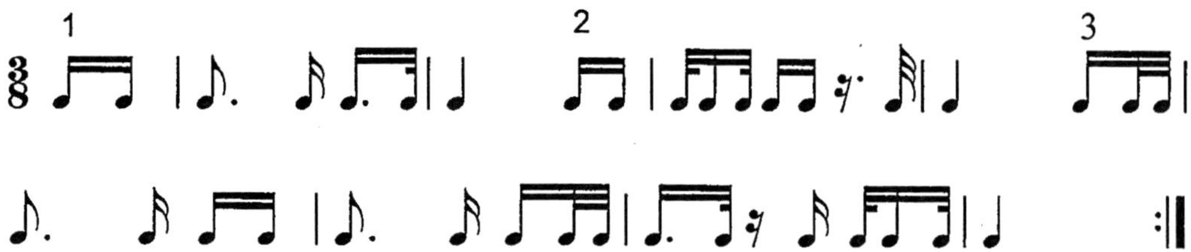

5.21 *Patience*, by Ariel d'Schelle

5.22 This example has a slow moving lower voice with quicker moving upper parts. It will help you practice reading rests in longer note values and count entrances at unusual parts of the beat. Notice the breve rests. On a lined staff they would fill the space between two line

5.23 Music isn't always written with beams connecting the beats. It is common especially in vocal music to see flags instead of beams, and unusual groupings based on the text. This exercise in the style of a vocal duet will give you more practice reading rhythm written with flags. Slurs in the upper voices indicate pitches that would be sung on a single syllable. These pitches may also connected with a beam. Be sure to look ahead as you read and look for the patterns. Be sure to distinguish the slurs from the ties.

6 ✧ Compound meter

Up to this point we have worked only with simple meters. Simple meters have beat notes that can be divided into two parts (*ta-di*) and have beat notes that are *not* dotted.

Compound meters have beat notes that divide into three parts at the first division. The beat notes in compound meter must therefore be dotted. (Review Chapter 1 for more on the theory of compound meter and meter signatures.)

First division of the beat

Just as in simple meter, the beat in compound meter is always on *ta*. But since we now have *three* equal divisions of the beat, we need new syllables. For this we use *ta-ki-da*.

There are only a few patterns we can make with *ta, ki,* and *da*. They are shown below with the dotted quarter as the beat. Write the patterns for the other beat notes. Be sure your notes are properly aligned.

♪. =beat	♩. = beat	𝅗𝅥. =beat	𝅝. =beat
ta	ta	ta	ta
ta ki da	ta ki da	ta ki da	ta ki da
ta da	ta da	ta da	ta da
ta ki	ta ki	ta ki	ta ki

Practice echo-rhythms with compound beats and first divisions before moving on to notation. Speak or clap short patterns and have a partner respond on syllables.

6.1

6.2 *Allegro ma non troppo*

6.3

6.4 *Con brio*

6.5

6.6

6.7 *Tranquille*

mp

6.8

Second Division of the Beat

The compound beat can also be divided a second time.

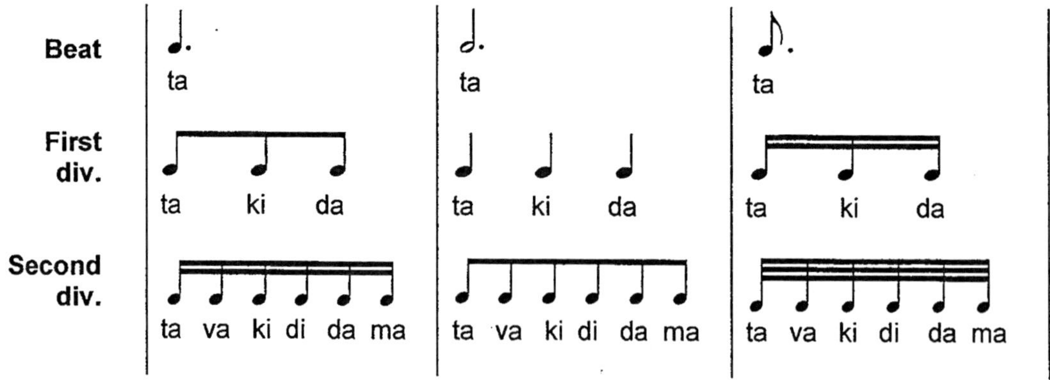

Dividing the compound beat a second time allows many more rhythmic possibilities. Following are six of the most common rhythmic patterns used in compound meter (shown with the dotted quarter note as the beat). Repeat each pattern to help you memorize it. Improvise short rhythms, incorporating these patterns gradually into ones you already know.

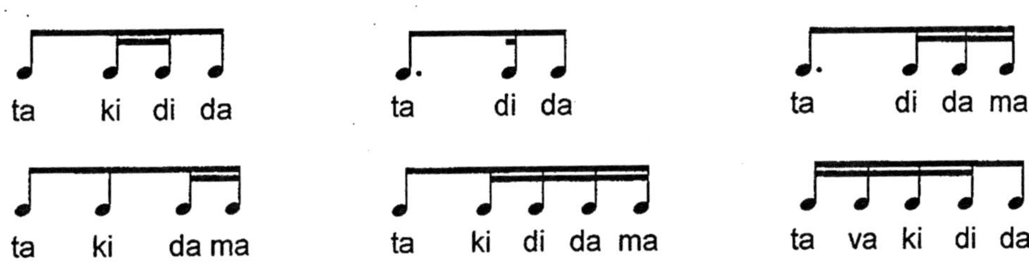

Practice echo-rhythms with these patterns before moving on.

6.11 Write each rhythm above the syllables. Line up each note with the second division of the beat *(ta-va-ki-di-da-ma)* at the top of the column. The first one is done for you.

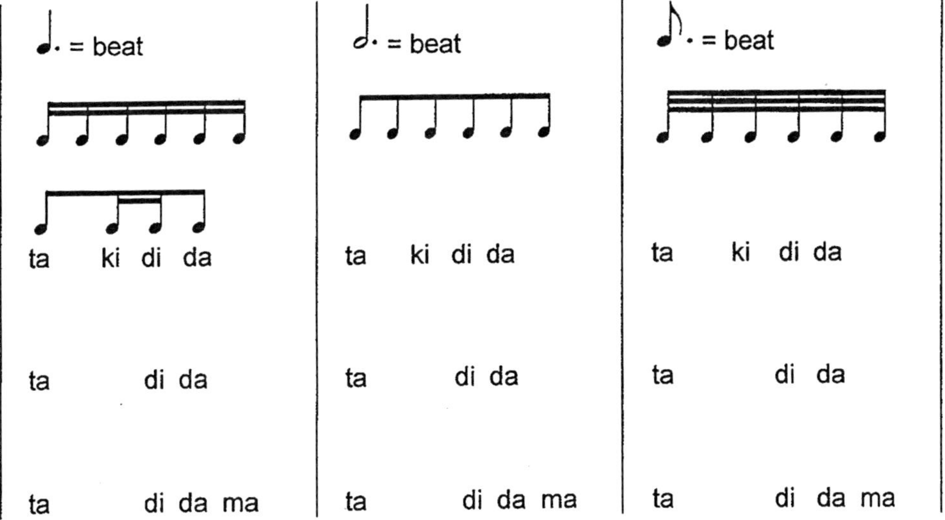

6.12 Write a second part to accompany the given rhythm. Include some second division patterns. Make sure the parts align properly. Perform your duet with a partner.

6.13 *Animato e con brio*

6.14 *Allegro ma non troppo*

6.15 *Con mosso*

6.16 ***Larghetto***

6.17 Perform each section at least twice. Change your improvisation each time. Also change your dynamics and articulation, but do so in a sensible and musical way.

6.18

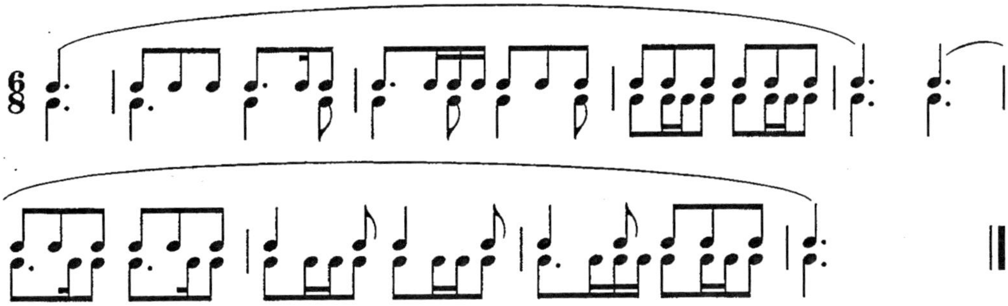

6.19 ***Lento*** (with improvisation measures)

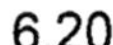

6.21 Write a second part to accompany the given rhythm. Be sure the parts align properly. Perform the exercise.

With longer beat notes, it is important to recognize the grouping even when you don't have the beams to guide you visually. As you practice, bracket and number the beats if it helps you see the patterns.

6.23 *Andantino*

f *mp*

mp *f* *mf*

mf

6.24 *Lightly*

6.25 ***Presto***

6.26 ***Andante moderato***

Metric groupings can be difficult to see in vocal music written with flags. Slurred and beamed notes indicate pitches that would be sung on a single syllable. Be sure to look ahead as you read. Bracket any beats that remain confusing.

6.27 ***Mässig***

Other less common patterns are introduced in the following exercises. Work out the syllables and practice the patterns before reading the exercise.

6.28

6.29 With improvisation measures

6.30

6.31 Leggiero
mp
pp
mp
senza rit.
6.32 Animato
6.33 Sempre piano e staccato
6.34 Maestoso (with improvisation measures)

6.35 Set the following text to rhythm in 6/4 meter. Be sure the accents in the text match the accents in the meter. Use proper notation.

Traditional rhyme

There was an old woman.

Lived under a hill;

And if she's not gone,

She lives there still.

6.36 "There Was an Old Woman" *Traditional rhyme*

6.37 ***Scherzando***

6.38

rit.

7 ✧ Ties in compound meter

Ties between beats make it especially important that you keep the beat in your head. Practice the exercises without the ties then with the ties, hearing the tied notes in your imagination. Syllables in parentheses show what you should first say, then think.

7.5

7.6 Try to include tied patterns in your improvisation.

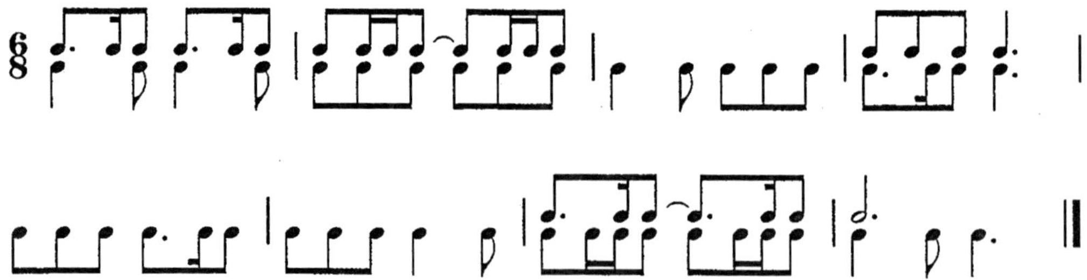

7.7 ***Sotto voce***

7.8 ***Grave***

mp

f

mp

rit.

7.9

(*f–p*)

(*f–p*)

7.10 ***Lively***

7.11 Canon. You may want to experiment with different timbres for the three parts. You may also wish to try different intervals of imitation, one beat, for example. Decide in advance how many times you will repeat the exercise.

7.12

7.13 Canon

7.14

7.15 ***Ruhig***

7.16 The older vocal style notation can make the metric groupings difficult to see. Bracket any measures that are unclear.

Hypermeter

In the first chapter we talked about the many levels of pulse that we can perceive and respond to. One level is called the beat. Beats can be grouped into measures and divided into divisions. Pulses that are a measure or longer can also be grouped to form larger patterns of strong and weak accents. This grouping above the measure level is called *hypermeter*. Hyper is a prefix meaning "above," so hypermeter is a metric grouping "above" the given or notated meter. The groupings are called hypermeasures.

Sing or chant "Over the River and Through the Woods." Conduct it as written in compound duple meter (for example, in 6/8).

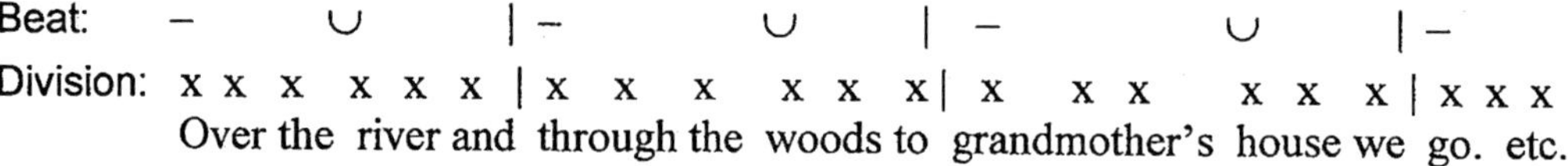

You can also group the measures into patterns of strong and weak accents that makes it sound like a very slow duple meter with measure twice as long as the original. Sing it again, this time conducting the slower hypermeasures.

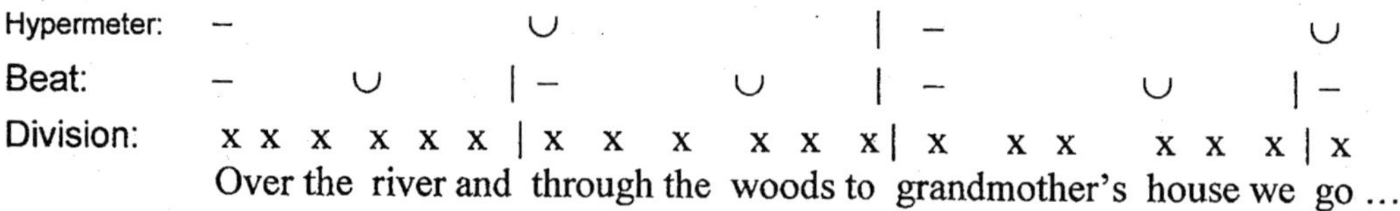

Hypermeter is very common in music, and affects our perception in a variety of ways. For example when we perform repeated measures louder then softer, we are treating those two measures as a strong and weak accents in a hypermeasure. Many styles of folk dance are based on hypermeter with steps repeated in patterns longer than the measure. You can probably think of many more tunes that can be regrouped in this way. Hypermeter can extend up to phrases and beyond, with entire phrases or even sections of pieces considered weak or strong in relation to others.

Hypermeter doesn't usually effect our performance or perception of the beat, except at quick tempos. Meters that look like simple triple (3/8 and 3/16 for example) can sometimes be thought of as compound duple at a level above the beat, especially at quicker tempos.

Perform the following in simple triple and again in compound duple. What are the musical differences? How would you decide which performance is correct or more appropriate? The placement of the cadence on the strong beat of the hypermeasure is often a factor, even at slower tempos.

7.17 ***Molto allegro***

In the chapters that follow evaluate examples in fast triple meter to determine how the beats should be grouped and conducted. Once you are aware of hypermeter, you may begin to hear it in all sorts of places.

8 ✧ Multiple dots, extended ties, third division

It is possible to place more than one dot on a note. Double, triple, and even quadruple dots are not uncommon. The first dot, as you know, adds one half the note value to the duration. Subsequent dots add half the value of the previous dot. For example:

Multiple dots sometimes make the beat hard to visualize. It may help to bracket or number the beats in a few examples until you are more comfortable with the notation.

8.1

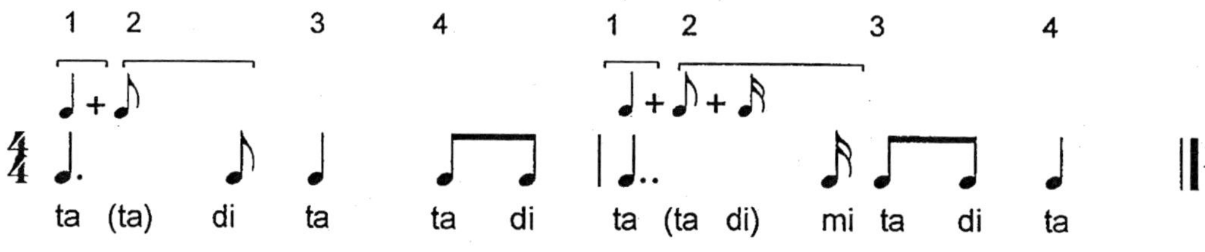

8.2

8.3 *Schnell*

8.4 The smaller notes above the first measure show the value of the triple dotted half note.

8.5

8.6 ***Spiritoso***

8.7 Conduct and count carefully. Follow the expression markings.

8.8 ***Triste***

8.9

8.10 Listen for which part has the "melody" and adjust your dynamics and articulation appropriately.

8.11 Rhythms may have divisions of the beat beyond the second division. There are no new syllables for these divisions. Instead you must change the beat level so that the smallest division is no more than a second division of the beat. Even though this example is written in 4/4, it is helpful to think of the eighth note as the beat. Syllables are shown below. In performance and once the rhythm is mastered, it might be appropriate to again feel the quarter note as the beat, depending on tempo and style.

8.12 More unusual are division so small that changing the beat becomes impractical. In this case it is usually easier to add a syllable—*ti* is suggested here—that helps you speak the rhythm accurately. These very small divisions often act as ornaments to a simpler, more familiar rhythm pattern. Here *ta-mi* is ornamented by dividing the *mi*. Sometimes you have to be creative in applying syllables.

8.13

8.14 *Larghetto*

8.15

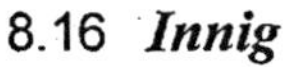

9 ✧ Syncopation and hemiola

At its most basic level, syncopation is a shifting of accent from a strong attack point—like a beat or strong beat—to another place in the measure, like an off beat or a normally weak beat. There are several ways to accomplish this shift. Accent signs, ties, or longer note values are three, and are among the techniques explored in this chapter. Other more complex techniques will be introduced later in the book.

9.4 After you learn the exercise, add one of more of the ostinatos as an accompaniment, or create your own. Listen for the composite rhythm and interaction among the parts.

ostinatos

9.5 *Accented*

9.6 *Expressive and sustained*

9.7 *Andante* (with improvisation measures)

f

Sometimes syncopation can occur in one part of the texture and not another. Or different parts can have conflicting syncopations. As you perform these multi-part exercises, be sure to consider the accent pattern of each part separately as well as how they interact. You may want to write in and listen for the composite rhythm.

9.8 ***Allegro maestoso***

9.9 ***Well marked***

9.10

mf

9.11

9.12 Compose a second part to accompany the rhythm. Think about the composite and how the added part will interact musically with the given part.

9.13 *Allegro con moto*

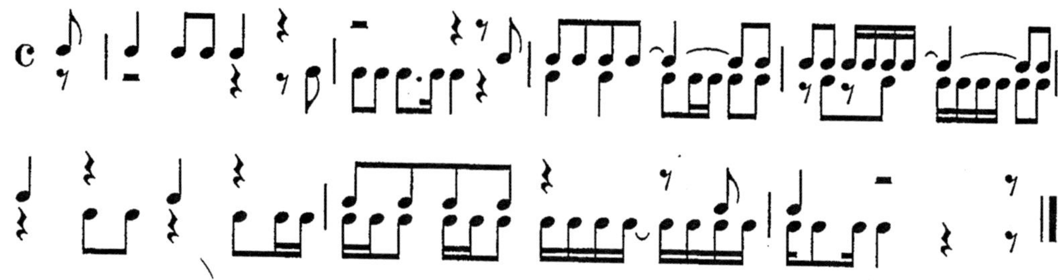

Hemiola

Hemiola is special form of syncopation describing the use of three even durations in place of two. It occurs in many forms throughout history. The following exercises show it in two of its most common forms, at the cadence and as regroupings within the measure of triple meter.

Rhythms like the following are common especially in music of the Baroque. Notice how the hemiola in measures 8 and 9 acts as a written retard to approach the cadence. You might even conduct these measures in 2 with a downbeat on each half note.

9.14 *Lively*

Hemiola in the next example is decorated a bit, but the regrouping into two is still evident. Bracket the groups of two in mm. 11 and 12. Even if you choose not to change your conducting pattern, be sure to accent the syncopated groupings.

9.15 ***Con mosso***

Sometimes hemiola runs throughout a piece. This is often the case when the six divisions in a measure of simple triple meter or compound duple meter are regrouped, as in the following exercise. (More examples will occur later in chapters on changing meter.)

9.16

9.17

9.18

9.19 Layer exercise. Listen for the accurate alignment of parts, especially involving the short notes following the double dotted notes.

9.20 With improvisation measures

9.21

The brackets in the last few measures suggest hemiola. Perform the exercise with and without the regrouping. How do the interpretations differ? Which do you like better?

9.22 *Allegro*

9.23 ***Schnell***

9.24 ***Cantabile***

9.25 This exercise is based on the piano accompaniment for a song by the 19th-century Austrian composer Hugo Wolf.

Langsam

9.26 This exercise is based on an excerpt from keyboard music written around 1570 by English composer Richard Farrant. Three separate lines are clear. Notice how the melodic and rhythmic patterns often seem to imply a meter other than 3/4 (mm. 2 and 3, for example). How might these groupings affect your performance?

10 ✧ Duplets and triplets

It is possible to divide the beat into three (*ta-ki-da*) in a simple meter. This division is called a triplet and is usually written with a "3" above the notes. Sometimes brackets are used to clarify the grouping. It is also possible to divide the beat into two parts (*ta-di*) in a compound meter. This pattern is called a duplet and is usually written with a "2" above the notes.

Look carefully at exercises 10.1 and 10.2. Notice that the rhythm syllables are exactly the same. A division of the beat into two is always spoken "*ta-di.*" A division into three is always "*ta-ki-da*" regardless of how the rhythm is written.

10.5 ***Largo***

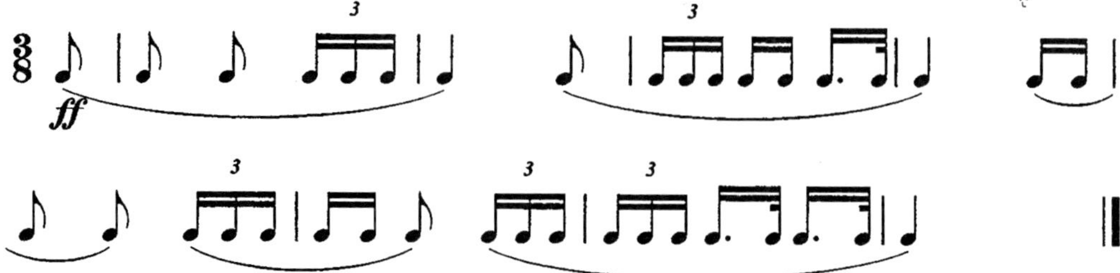

10.6 ***Allegro e resoluto***

10.7

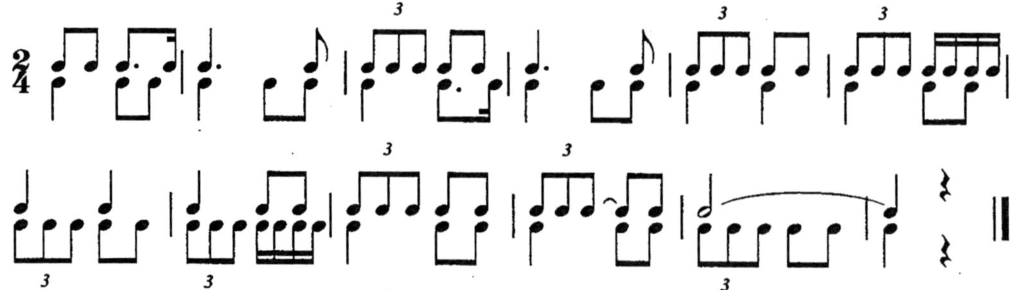

10.8 Duplets and triplets can be further subdivided. Here the duplet is divided into four, or *ta-ka-di-mi*.

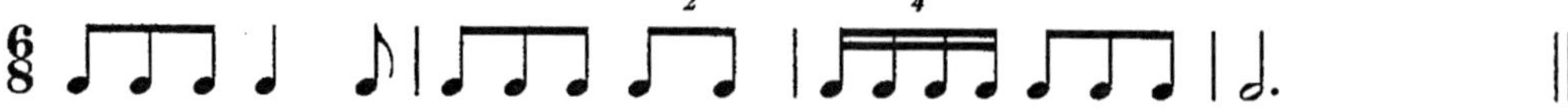

10.9 The division into six can be thought of as a division of the beat into six parts (m. 3), or making a triplet from each division (m. 4). In either case the syllables are the same, *ta-va-ki-di-da-ma,* although in the second instance you might accent *ta* and *di*.

10.10

10.11 With improvisation measures.

10.12 The duplet division may also be written in another way, as shown in the exercise below.

10.13 *Leggiero*

10.14 *Lento*

10.15 *Moderato*

10.16

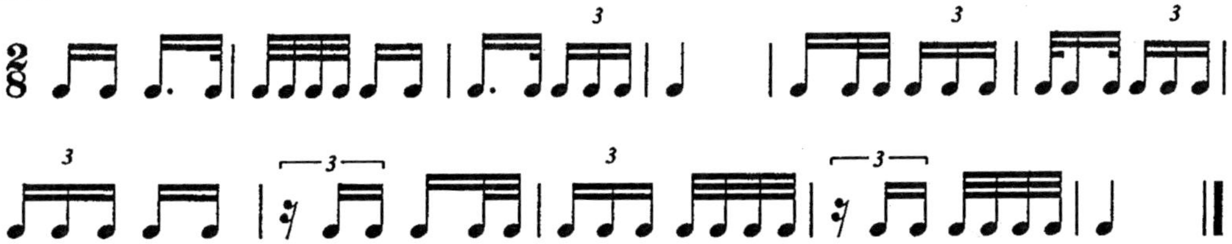

10.17 *Energico*

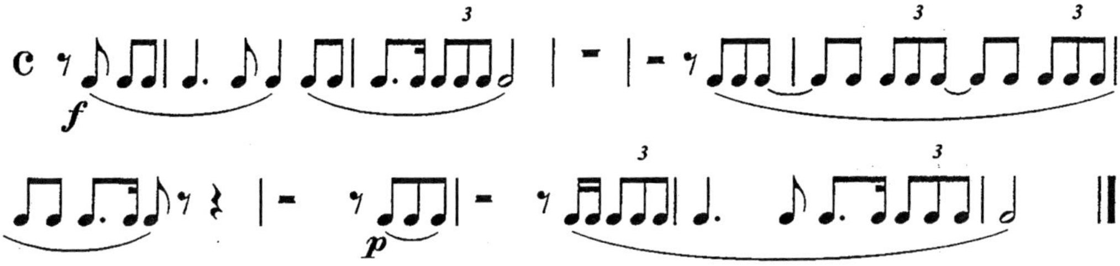

f *p*

10.18 *Piacevole*

f *mp* *f*

10.19

10.20 With improvisation measures.

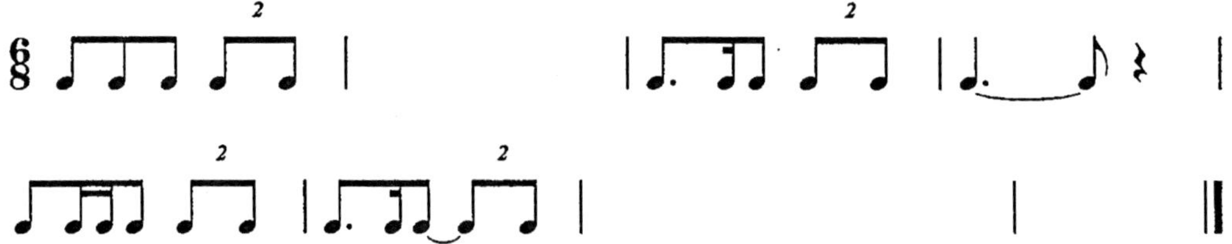

10.21

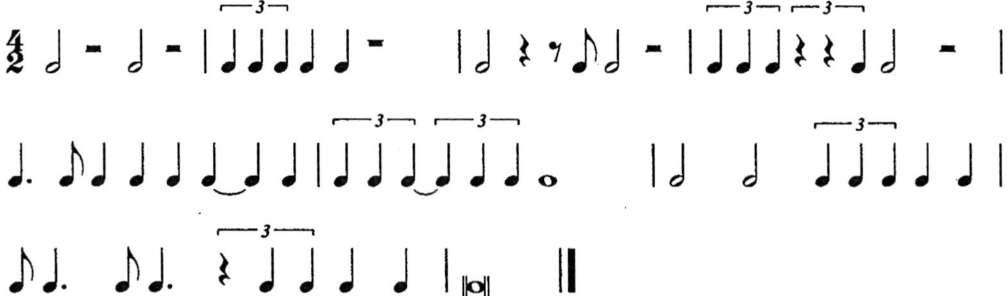

10.22 *Lebhaft*

11 ✧ Two against three

"Two against three" involves performing duplets and triplets at the same time or "against" each other. In this chapter we will consider only duplets and triplets within a single beat. In Chapter 15 we will learn about duplets and triplets that span more than one beat.

Notice that *ta* and *di* align the beginning and mid-points of the beat, in both simple and compound divisions. Aligning *di* will help us perform these rhythms accurately.

Practice speaking one part and clapping the other. Pay close attention to the alignment of *ta* and *di*.

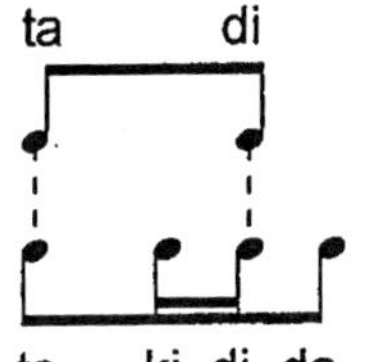

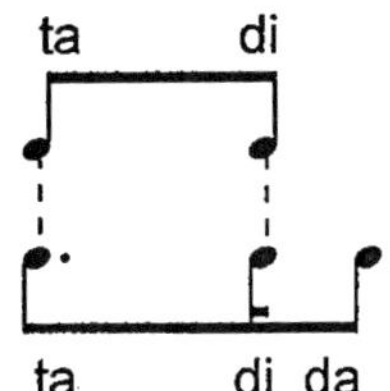

When we perform both divisions together, we hear the composite rhythm "*ta-ki-di-da*."

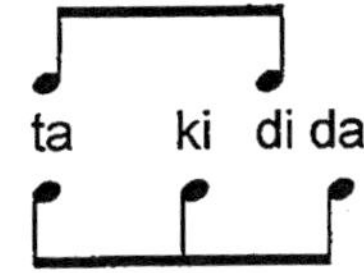

Practice with these patterns, and other similar ones you create, until you can speak and clap two against three accurately and readily.

11.1 Repeat each measure until the pattern is secure. Perform the measures in different combinations. Listen for the *ta-ki-di-da* composite in each measure.

11.2 Write the composite rhythm between the staves, then listen for the composite rhythm to emerge as you perform the exercise. (You may want to write the composite rhythms in other exercises as well.)

11.3 Repeat several times, changing parts, dynamics, and articulations. Always listen for the *ta-ki-di-da* composite rhythm.

11.4 ***Poco adagio***

11.5

11.6

3

3

3

3

11.7 *Lively*

2 2

2 2 2

2 2

11.8 Write the composite rhythm between the staves.

2

2

2 2

2 2

11.9

11.10

11.11 *Lebhaft*

11.12

11.13 Try to incorporate at least one duplet in your improvisation measures.

11.14 *Allegro ma non troppo*

3 3

3 3 3

11.15 *Pesante*

2 2 2 2

11.16 *Nicht zu schnell*

3

3 3

3

3 3 3

3 3

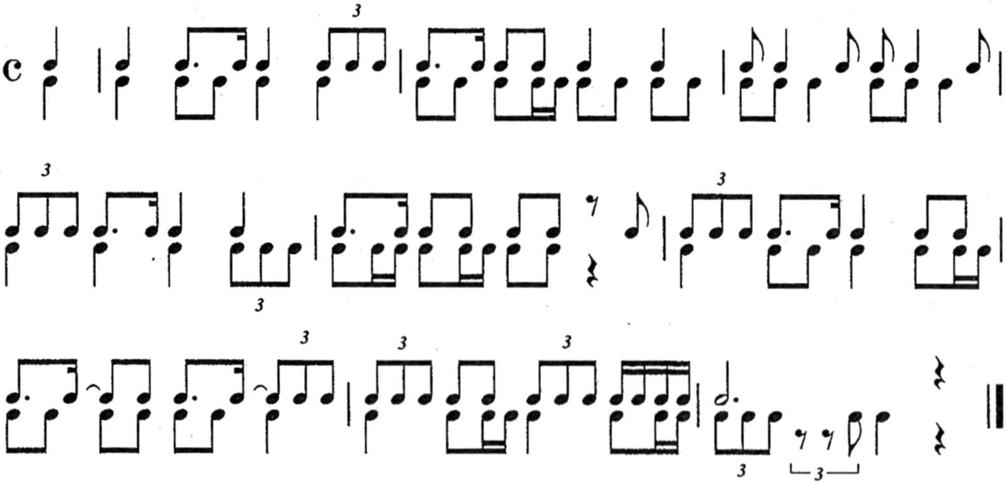

12 ✧ Changing meter I — Regrouping beats

Changing meter is one effective way to change accent patterns. There are many possible relationships among meters. Exercises in this chapter maintain a constant duration for both the beat and the division of the beat. Only the metric grouping change (like duple to triple). In Chapters 13 and 14 we will explore meter changes where the length of the beats and divisions changes.

Conducting is especially important when performing changing meter. Practice changing meter and your conducting patterns in the following exercise. Count the beats in the measure as you go. Notice the "courtesy" or "cautionary meter signature" at the end of the first line. This warns the reader that the next line begins with a meter change.

12.4

12.5

12.6 Rewrite the rhythm, changing the written meter so that the accented notes fall on downbeats. What are advantages to each way of writing it?

While the "alla breve" symbol ("C-slash") usually indicates 2/2, it can also indicate any meter with the half note as the beat. Look ahead to read the changing meter in the following exercise.

12.7

12.8

12.9 *Lively*

12.10 With improvisation measures.

12.11 ***Scherzando***

Notice the symbol in the text above the meter change. This indicates that the duration of the quarter note in 4/4 will equal the duration of the half note in 3/2. In other words the beat note remains the same in length, but the notation changes from quarter note to half note.

12.12 ***Dolce***

12.13

12.14 ***Stark***

12.15

f mp f f mp mp f f f

12.16 Improvise or compose a clapping or percussion part to complement the rhythm.

12.17

13 ✧ Changing meter II — Equal beats

The more common relationship between meters keeps the beat the same length. But if the meter changes between simple and compound, the length of the *division* will change. To illustrate this, complete the written exercise below.

13.1 Write in the rhythm syllables, and perform the example.

Now, rewrite the example, changing the meter for measures 2 and 3. Write in the rhythm syllables and perform this example.

Finally rewrite the entire example in 6/8 *without* changing meter. Use duplets for the duple divisions. Write in the rhythm syllables and perform this example.

In all three cases the length of the beat remains the same length, but the length of the division—the eighth note—changes. (The syllables should remain the same as well.)

In the following example, the dotted quarter note beat in 6/8 will be equal in length to the quarter note beat in 2/4. The two eighth notes in 2/4 will sound like a duplet in 6/8, and the triple division of the beat in 6/8 will sound like a triplet in relation to 2/4.

13.2 Think about how the change of meter will affect the tempo after the change. It is possible that a tempo appropriate for one section will be too fast or too slow after the meter changes.

13.3 *Adagio*

13.4

13.5 *Allegro*

(♩ = ♩.)

2

2

13.6 *Lively*

(𝅗𝅥 = 𝅗𝅥.)

13.7 *Allegro* (with improvisation measures)

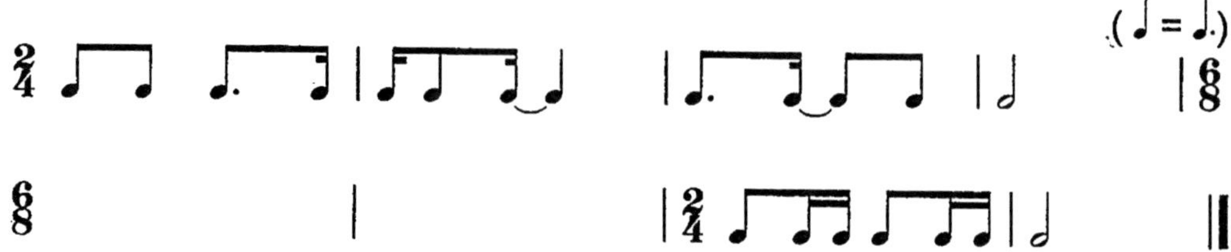

13.8 Perform as a canon in two or three parts, entering where indicated. Listen for the pattern of accents to change as the meters interact.

13.9 *Lively*

The relationship between meters is not always shown. In the following exercise, the use of triplets in the simple meter sections strongly suggests the beat will stay the same.

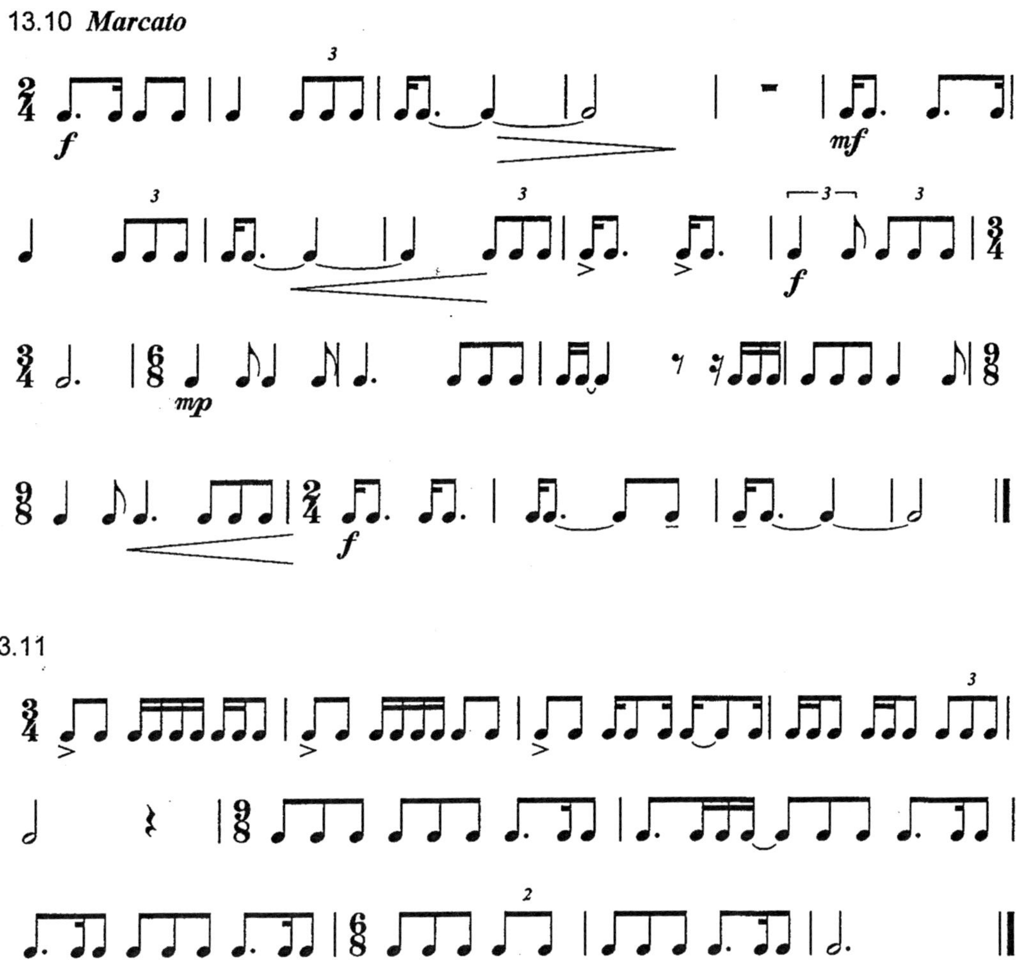

13.12 *Sotto voce e dolce*

marcato

13.13

mf

(♩. = ♩) *sempre leggiero*

mp

3

3

3

3

13.14
13.15 Vif

* In Greek mythology, Erebus is a region of Hades and sometimes refers to Hades itself.

14 ✧ Changing meter III — Equal divisions

In the last chapter we saw changes of meter with the beat remaining equal. Another option is to keep the divisions equal. Of course this will make the beats unequal. Perform these examples until you are comfortable with the differences.

14.1 Equal Beats

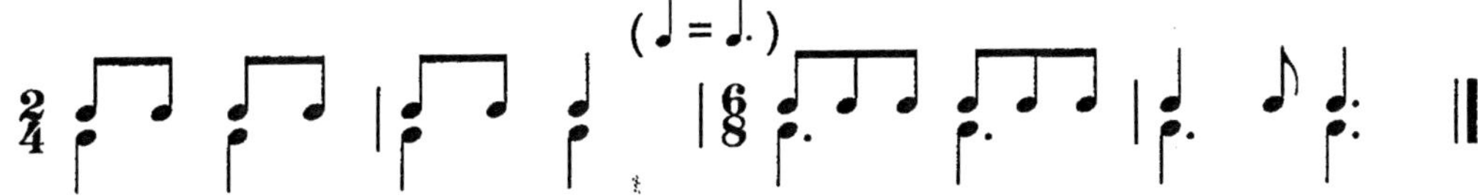

14.2 Equal Divisions

Look carefully at the notation in each example to determine the relationship of the beat and division. Practice the change by speaking and clapping the beats and divisions as you did for the previous examples. What does *sempre* indicate in this exercise?

14.3

14.4

14.5

(♪ = ♪)

14.6

(♪ = ♪ *sempre*)

Compare examples 14.7 and 14.8 carefully. How are they different? How will the durations change?

14.7

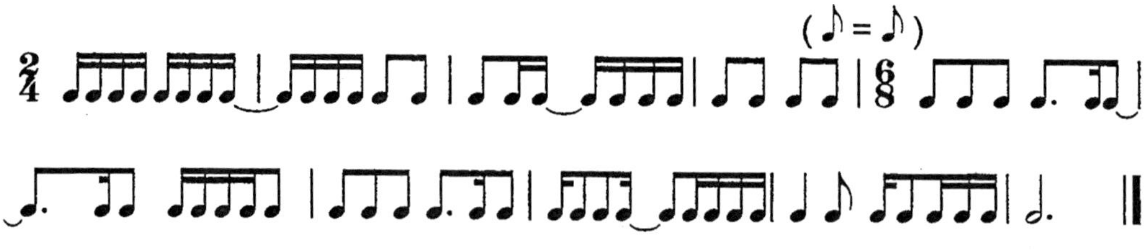

(♪ = ♪)

14.8

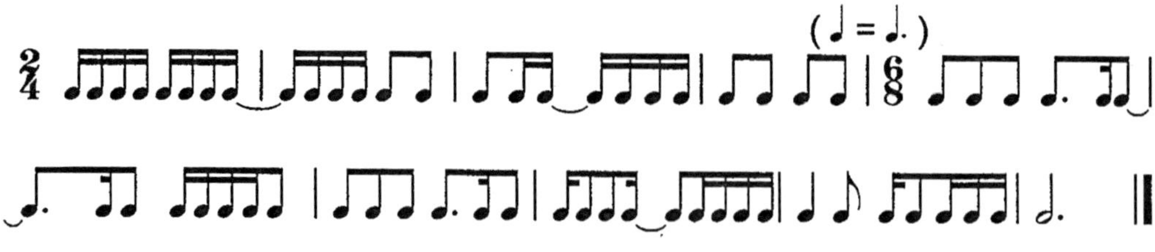

(♩ = ♩.)

14.9

(♪ = ♪)

14.10

(♪ = ♪)

(♪ = ♪)

(♪ = ♪)

14.11 *Allegro assai*

(♩ = ♩.)

14.12

(♩ = ♩)

14.13 *Marcato*

(♩ = ♩)

(♩ = ♩.)

14.14 *Ziemlich stark*

14.15

14.16 Perform this rhythmic poem two different ways, with both the beats equal and the divisions equal. Which do you prefer and why?

Iroquois song, Anonymous

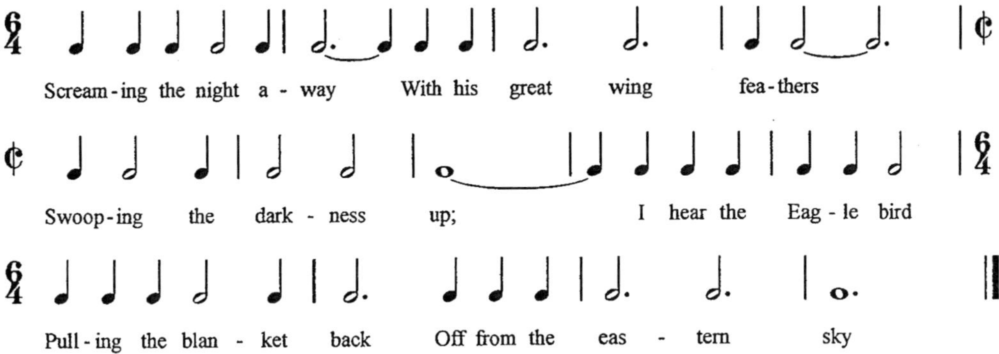

14.17 In this example performers would most certainly keep the quarter note constant. In this case the division appears to equal the beat. But perhaps the 4/4 sections should be thought of as 2/2. In that case the division stays constant. Could it make a difference in how the music is performed? Music notation is amazing in what it can communicate, but it still leaves lots of room for ambiguity and interpretation.

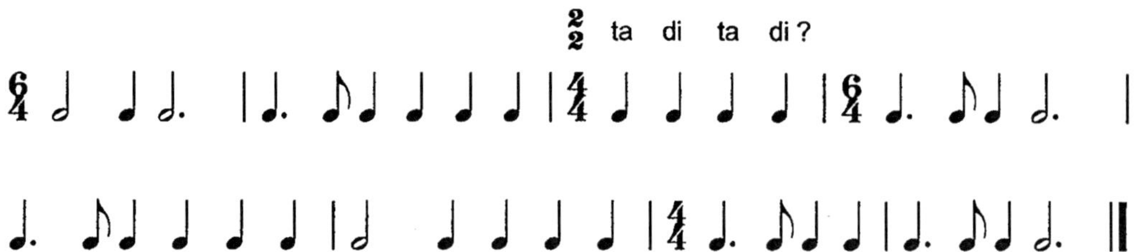

14.18

14.19

15 ✧ Superduplets and supertriplets

The term *tuplet* is used for any even, irregular division of a pulse. We have already studied the most common tuplets: duplets and triplets. *Superduplets* and *supertriplets* are duplets and triplets that extend across two or more beats. We will study irregular divisions into five and seven parts—quintuplets and septuplets—in Chapter 16.

Key to performing any tuplet accurately is sensing the equal division of pulse being divided. Finding the correct syllables for the underlying attack points will help you do that. In this example, the superduplet aligns with *ta* and *di* of the simple division of the beat. Experiment by speaking the division of the beat, and clapping the duplet on *ta* and *di*, or have part of the class speak the background while others speak the duplet.

15.1

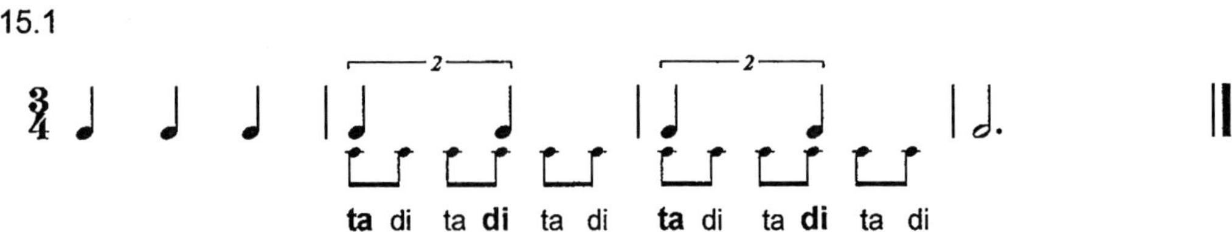

15.2 Perform this first while conducting or clapping the beat, and then add the written clapping part. Practice at different tempos. Listen for the alignment on *ta* and *di*. Listen too for the composite rhythm produced by the two lines.

15.3 Write a superduplet and a quarter note above each measure. Align the notes carefully. Write the composite rhythm syllables between the lines. Perform the rhythm as a speak and clap or a duet.

15.5 Because the superduplet lines up with regular divisions of the beat, there are several ways to write the rhythm. In the following examples the superduplet rhythm is written without the duplet sign. Can you find it?

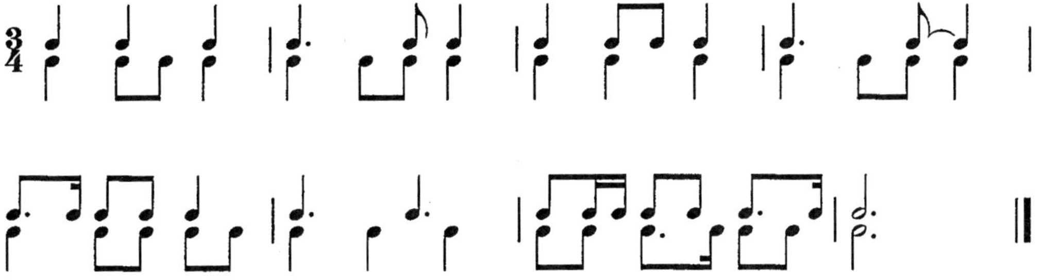

15.6

15.7 Supertriplets are triplets that span two or more beats. It is useful to think about the underlying compound division of the beat even in simple meter. These two examples would sound identical even though they are notated differently.

a.

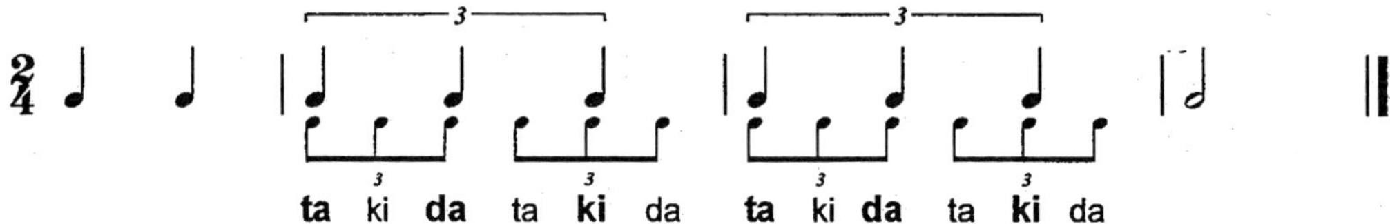

b. The triplet over two beats in compound meter is a regrouping of the regular division of the beat, and is very similar to a type of hemiola studied in chapter 9. If the division is clear, it is usually not necessary to write the triplet sign.

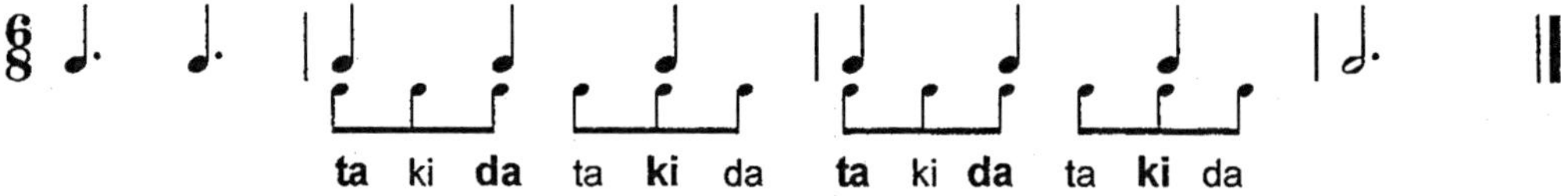

15.8 Here is an example of hemiola. In what other ways could this exercise be notated? Write some options on the score.

Because of the common elements, rhythms like those in this chapter challenge our concept of simple and compound meter. In later chapters we will look at examples best understood as using simple and compound at the same time, a technique called "polymeter." Notice how often you have to change your thinking from simple to compound as you continue working in this chapter.

15.9

15.10 Write a supertriplet in each measure. Write the composite rhythm syllables between the lines.

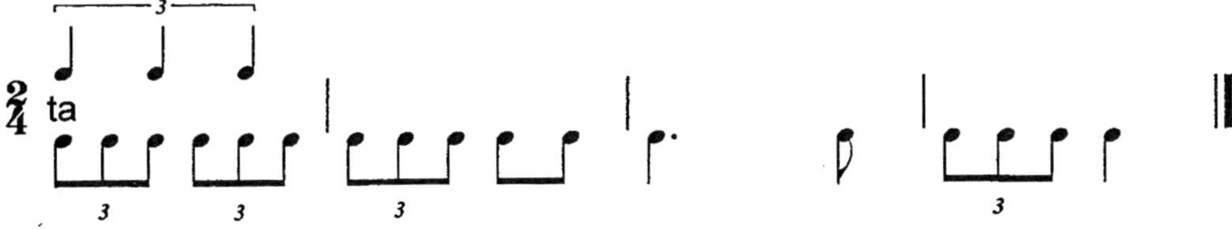

15.11 *En allant*

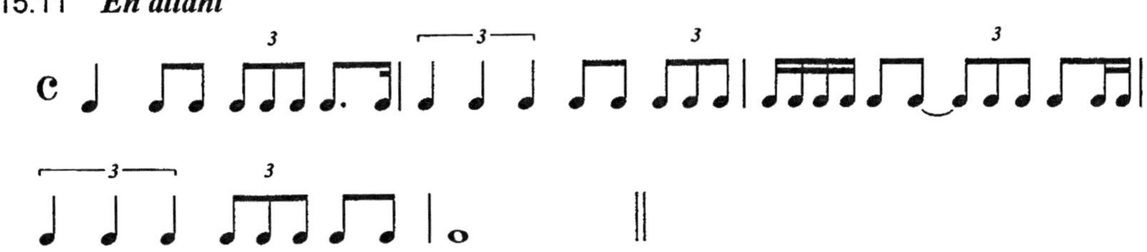

15.12 With the changing meter and the tuplets, it may be better in this example to think of the quarter note as the beat. Write in the division and the syllables for each tuplet. The first one is done for you. Keep the quarter note constant.

15.13

15.14

15.15

15.16

15.17 Write a complementary clapping part below the given line. Be sure to align the notes properly. Write the composite rhythm syllables between the lines.

clap:

15.18 With improvisation measures.

15.19

15.20 What is the relationship between the parts on the third line? After learning the rhythm, you may wish to sing this example on pitch.

16 ✧ Irregular divisions of the beat

So far we have looked at the most common divisions of the beat into two (*ta-di*) and three (*ta-ki-da*), and subdivisions into four (*ta-ka-di-mi*) and six (*ta-va-ki-di-da-ma*). Theoretically beats can be divided into any number of divisions or subdivisions.

Of the many possibilities, irregular divisions into five and seven, called quintuplets and septuplets, are perhaps most common. So that we don't have to learn whole new sets of syllables for these unusual patterns, we will modify the syllables we already know. As you practice, take care to keep the division even. It is easy for irregular divisions to "swing" or get bunched up near the beginning or end of the beat if you are not careful. We will study irregular divisions over more than one beat in Chapter 20.

16.1 Be sure to keep the quintuplet even. Clap, conduct, or step to the beat.

16.4

16.5 *Allegro ma non troppo*

(♩. = ♩)

(♩ = ♩.)

16.6 *Mesto ma non troppo*

16.7 In this example fill in the blanks with an even division of the beat.

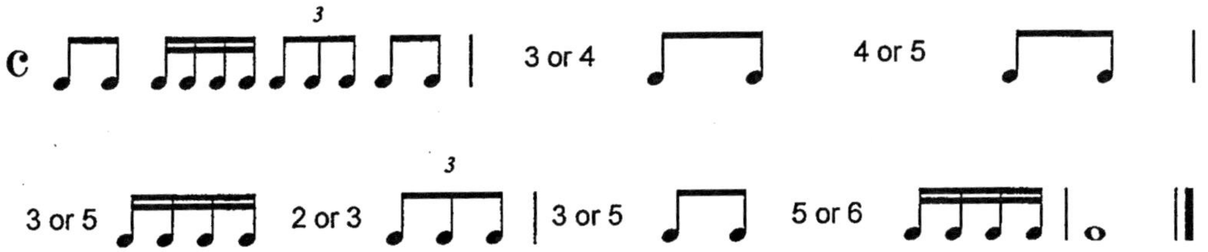
3 or 4
4 or 5
3 or 5
2 or 3
3 or 5
5 or 6

16.8

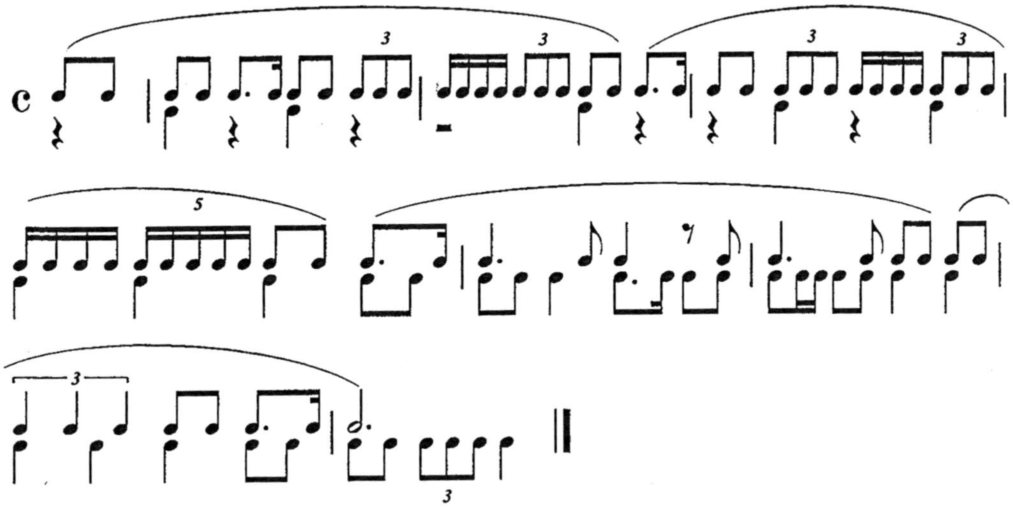

The other most common irregular divisions are septuplets, or divisions of the beat into 7 parts. As with quintuplets we will modify syllables we already know.

16.9

ta ta di ta va ki di da ma ti ta di

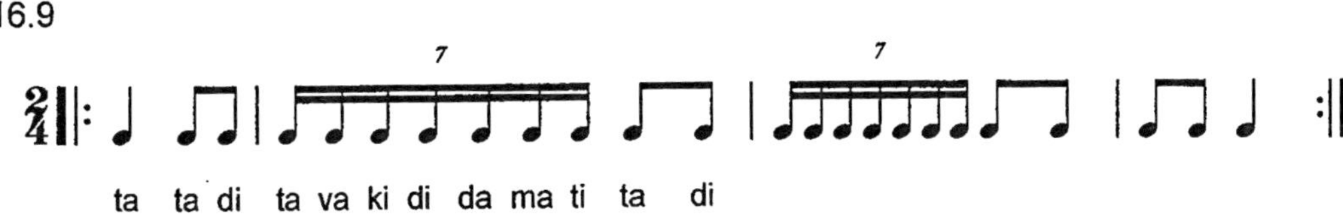

Even though we are using the familiar syllables it is important to note that the same syllables no longer line up. The *di* in *ta-ka-di-mi* and the *di* in *ta-ka-di-mi-ti* or in *ta-va-ki-di-da-ma-ti* are *not* at the same point in time. Unlike regular divisions into two, three, four, or six parts, quintuplets and septuplets have no common attack points except *ta*. This is in part what makes divisions into five and seven "irregular" and beyond what we normally encounter in tonal music.

16.10

16.11

16.12 Because there are no common syllables to help align the parts, each part in the following duets must maintain an independent and even division of the beat.

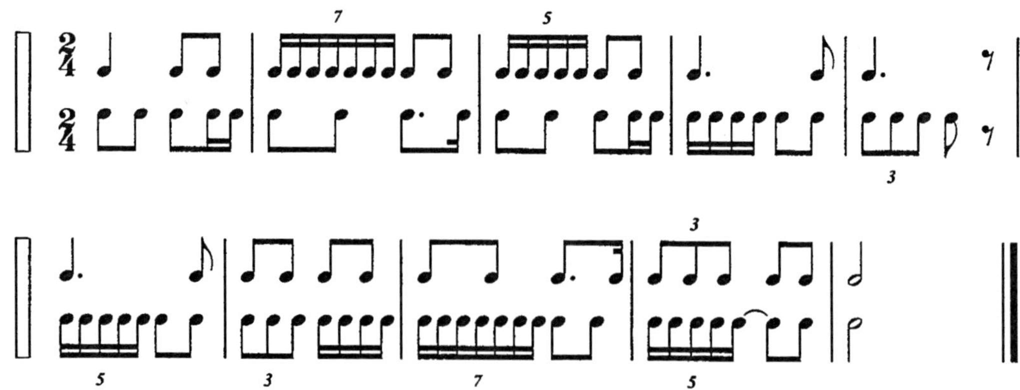

17 ✧ 4:3 relationships

"Four to three" relationships are closely related to the superduplets and supertriplets we studied in Chapter 15. The two most common relationships are the supertriplet over the span of four beats and the superquadruplet over the span of three beats. These are easier to see in pictures than explain in words.

Shown below are four even pulses (the superquadruplet) spread across three beats.

It aligns with the subdivision of the beats on the syllables *ta-mi-di-ka.*

The middle line shows the composite rhythm produced by the quadruplet and the beat.

As you perform the following exercises listen for the composite rhythm produced by the interaction of the lines, or in the case of single line exercises, the interaction of the tuplet with the underlying beat.

The following exercises provide two ways to begin to hear the superquadruplet over three beats. First do the exercise as a duet. Listen for the composite rhythm produced by the interaction of the two parts. Then do the exercise by speaking the top line and clapping the bottom line. Again, listen for the composite rhythm.

17.1 Repeat each section as often as necessary. Write in the composite rhythm if it helps you see the relationship. It should be the same for each measure.

17.2 Repeat each section as often as necessary to become familiar with the interaction between parts and the resulting composite. Strive for independence between parts and the ability to listen to each part as you perform.

17.3 This exercise introduces variations of the 4:3 composite rhythm in mm. 1 – 3 to help prepare for the superquadruplet in m. 4.

17.4

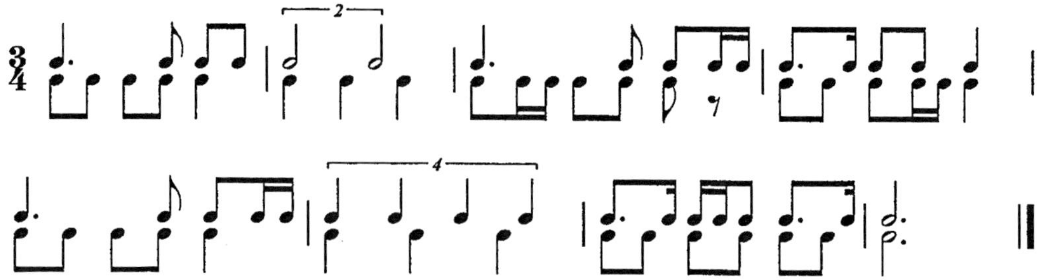

17.5 Layer exercise — Decide in advance or follow a leader's direction regarding how many times you will repeat each section and when each part will enter. Listen for the interaction between parts, especially the composite rhythm produced by the quadruplet.

17.6 Create an improvisation in the blank measures that complements the rhythm of the supertuplet.

17.7

Another 4:3 relationship involves a supertriplet across four beats. You may want to review the triplet within the beat (*ta-ki-da*) and the triplet over two beats (*ta-da-ki*) before continuing.

The supertriplet aligns with the divisions of the beat on the syllables *ta-ki-da*, just as a one-beat triplet.

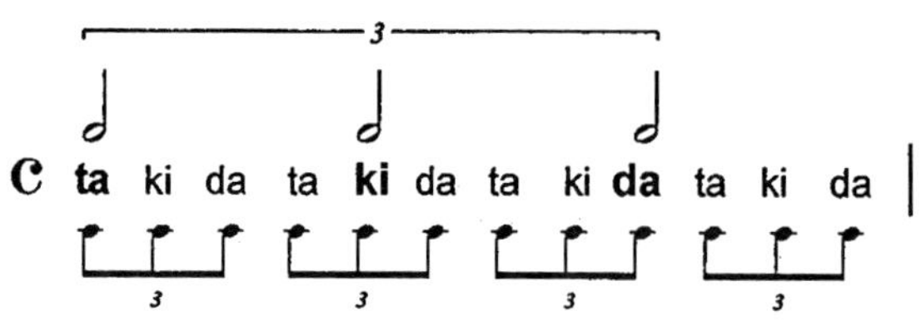

The composite of the triplet and the underlying beat notes then is shown.

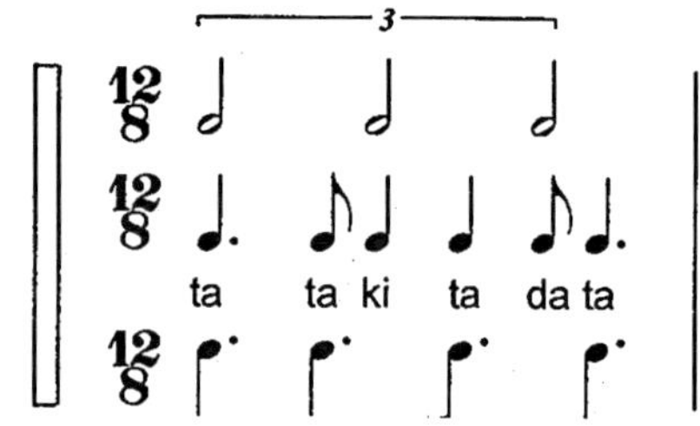

Notice in the above, the example on the left is notated in a simple meter and the one on the right is notated in compound. There is no difference in the sound of the supertriplet or the syllables used. The divisions of the underlying beat could be written either as triplets in simple meter or as the normal divisions of the beat in compound. Keep this in mind as you study the following examples.

17.8 Repeat each section as often as necessary. Listen for the composite rhythm.

17.9 Repeat each section as often as necessary. Listen for the composite rhythm.

17.10 Conduct or clap the beat.

17.11 Even in simple meter use the compound division of the beat for the supertriplet. Listen for the composite rhythm.

17.12

17.13

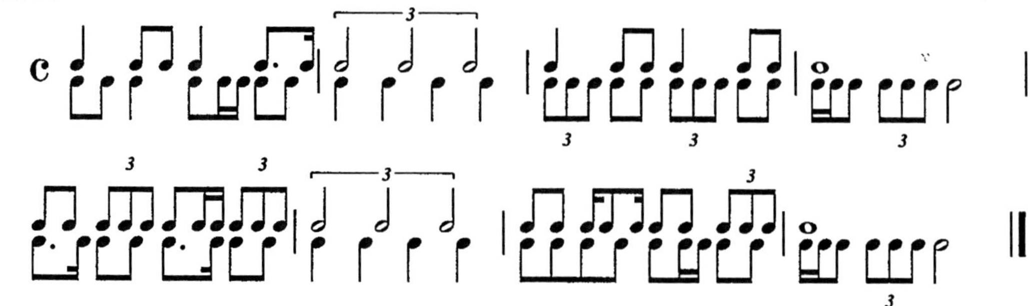

17.14

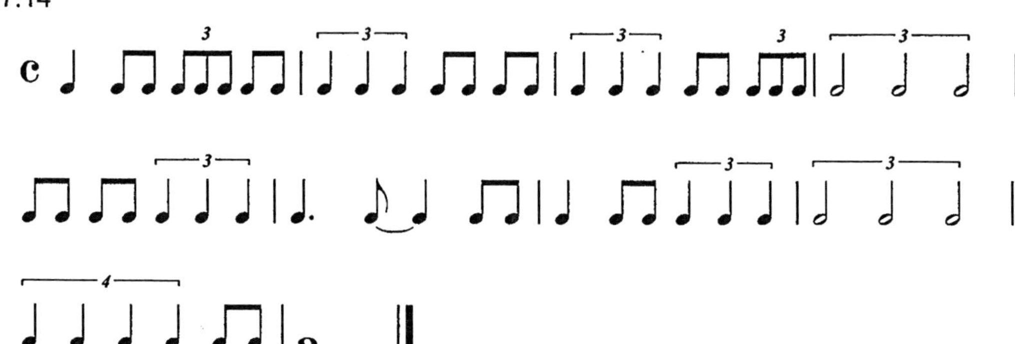

17.15 The supertriplet in the following example is notated in three different ways. Find all three and explain why they are all accurate ways to represent the same sound.

f

12/8

12/8

mp

f

3

3

18 ✧ Asymmetric meters — 5 and 7 divisions

Asymmetric meters have beats of different lengths, or put another way, beat notes that do not divide into the same number of divisions. Most common are measures that have five or seven divisions in a measure.

Asymmetric meters are a bit like compound meters in that the meter signature shows us how many divisions of the beat are in a measure, but not how many beats. We must group the divisions to determine the beats. Meters with five divisions usually have two beats grouped by two and three. Often the grouping is made clear by the notation (mm. 1 – 4), but sometimes it is not (m. 5). You may conduct these examples in two, but the beats will not be the same length. If the tempo is very slow, the music may give the effect of changing meter, with the groupings of two and three actually being groupings of two and three beats. The following exercise at a slow tempo might sound like alternating 3/8 to 2/8, for example. Perform it at both a fast and slow tempo. What is the difference in the way you perceive the meter?

18.1

Perform the following example clapping the lower line, and then conducting the beat. Alternate these two methods of performance and repeat until you are comfortable with the unequal beat lengths.

18.2

18.3

18.4

Sometimes the grouping is made explicit by the meter signature. These are called composite meter signatures. Notice in this example the rhythm in m. 5 is not ambiguous. (See ex. 18.1, m.5.)

18.5

18.7 Write an upper part to complement the lower line given. Be sure your groupings match those in the lower voice.

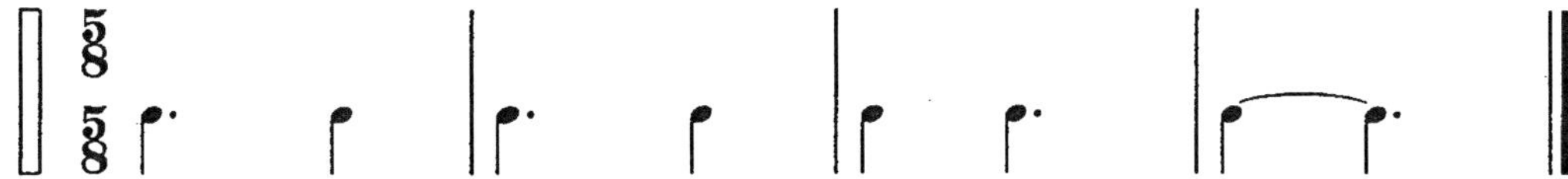

18.8 ***Andante*** (with improvisation measures)

18.9 After you learn the rhythm, improvise an appropriate clapping part.

18.10

Seven divisions in a measure present even more options for grouping. Groupings are still most often by twos and threes, and there are usually three beats in a measure.

18.11

3 + 2 + 2 3 + 2 + 2 2 + 3 + 2 2 + 2 + 3

18.12

18.13

18.14 Compose an upper part that complements the lower line. Your grouping may match the given voice or it may conflict with it. Either way, be sure your notation is correct.

Transcribe both parts into 7/4.

18.15 Notice that the grouping are not the same in the two parts. Make the beats well accented as you perform. Bracket the beats in any measure where the notation is unclear.

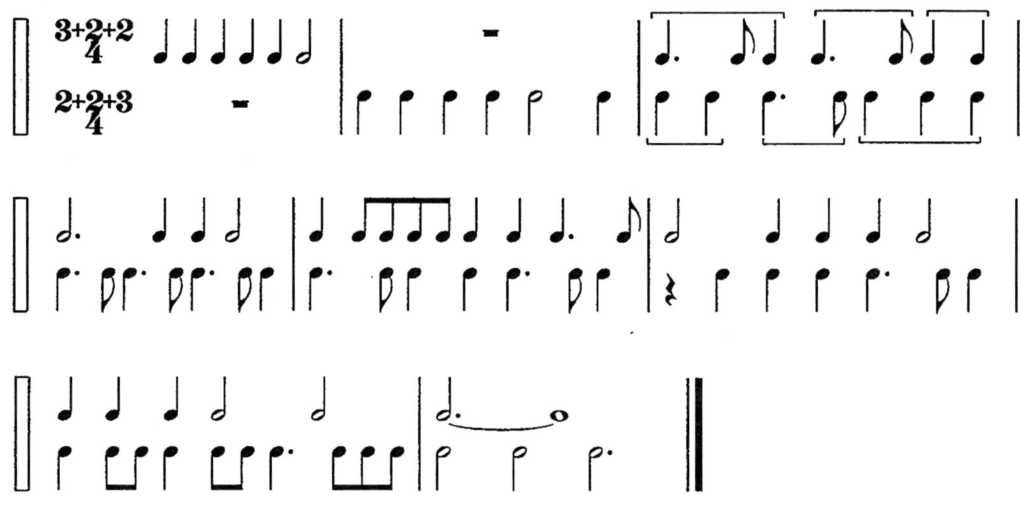

18.16 *Lent*

18.17

18.18 With improvisation measures.

18.19 ***So schnell wie möglich***

19 ✧ Asymmetric meters II — Other unusual groupings

A variety of asymmetric meters and unusual beat divisions are possible in music. This chapter explores some of the options.

19.1 The irregular grouping of 8 divisions as 3+3+2 is actually fairly common in popular music and music for television.

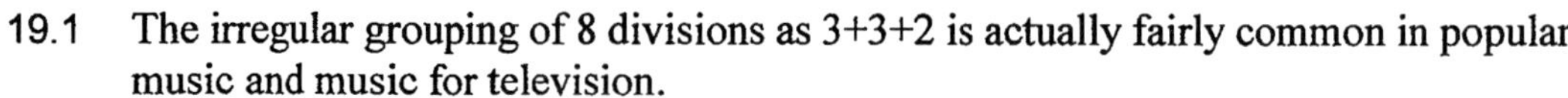

19.2 Compose a rhythm that fits the given meter. Be sure to notate it in a way the shows the groupings. Perform your rhythm.

19.3 Sometimes meters that appear regular can be grouped irregularly. Don't mistake these regroupings for duplets or triplets. The division of the beat—in this case the eighth note—should remain constant. Accents on *ta* will make the grouping clear.

19.4 *Allegro con brio*

19.5 In this example further division of the beat makes it possible to think of the example as mixed meter, with groupings indicated by the dashed line.

19.6 How will the triplets in m. 3 sound different from the three eighth notes in the same measure? The syllables will be the same. What will change? Clap the beats.

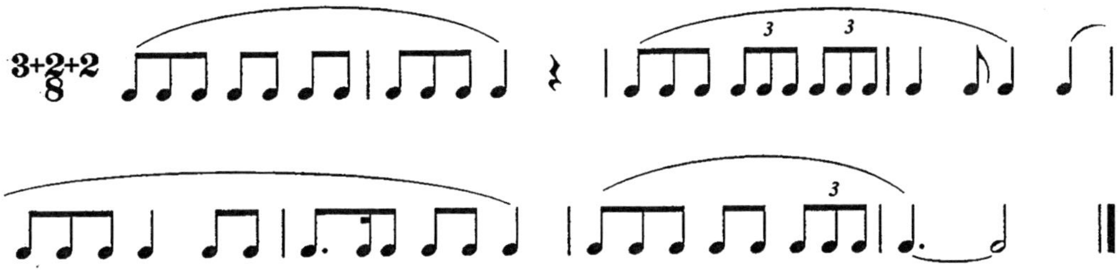

19.7

19.8

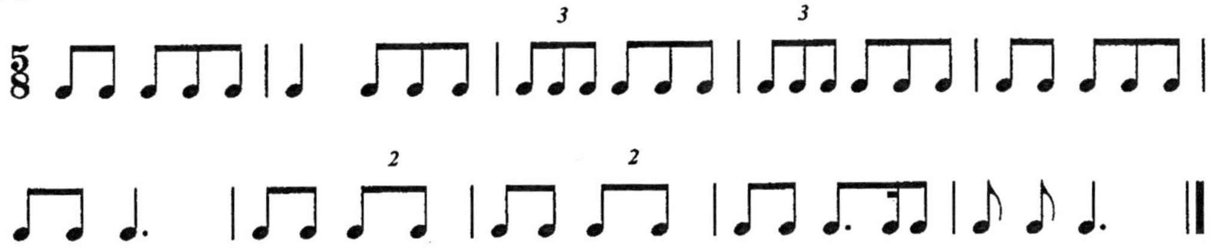

19.9

19.10

19.11

19.12

19.13 Both the notation and the music allow for a variety of groupings. Keep the quarter note constant, but make purposeful and musical decisions about groupings. Be sure your performance is expressive.

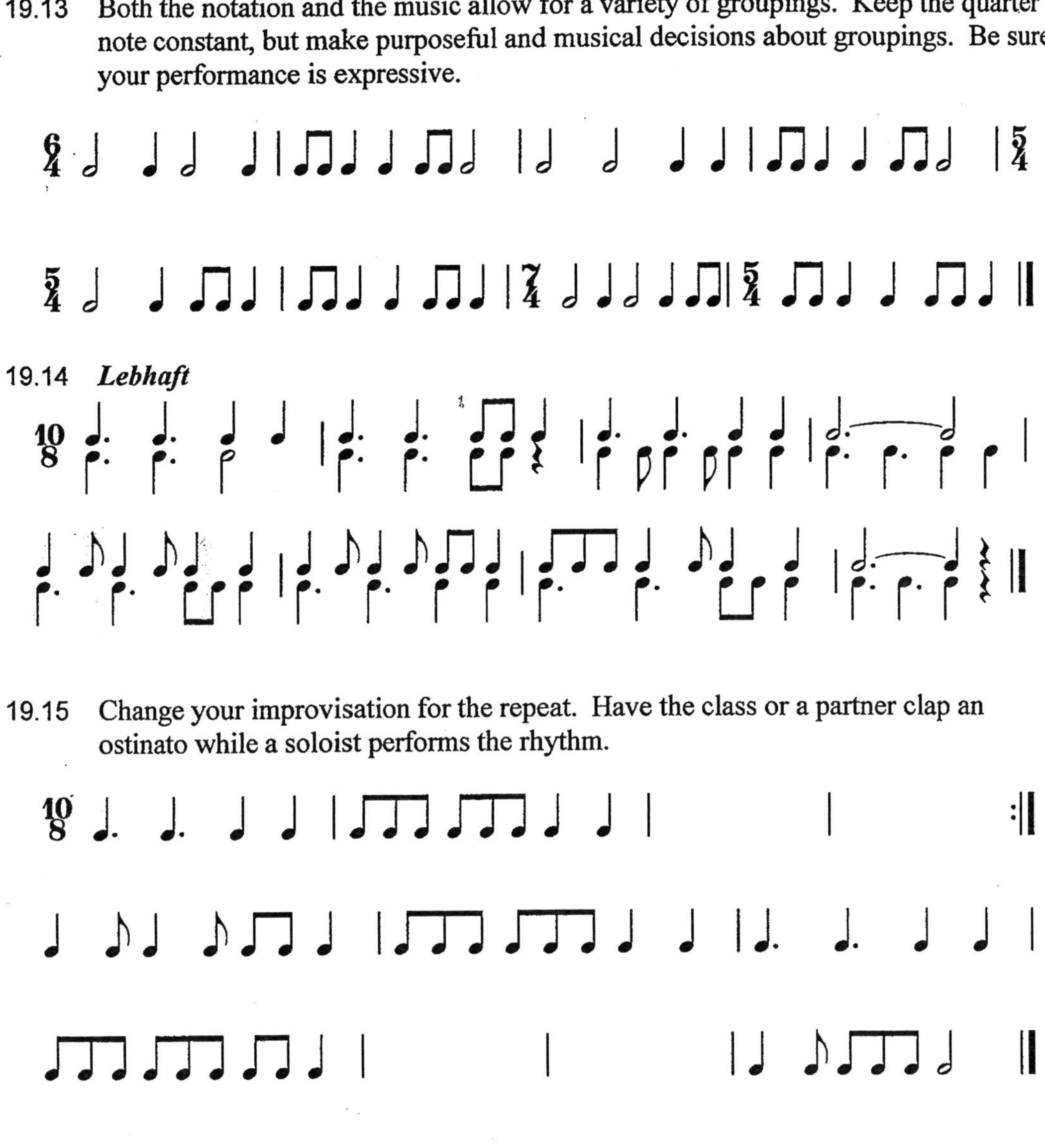

19.15 Change your improvisation for the repeat. Have the class or a partner clap an ostinato while a soloist performs the rhythm.

19.16 Be sure to accent the first notes of the groupings. What is the relationship of the upper and lower parts?

19.17

Bracketing the groups might make the rhythm easier to read and to learn, especially where there is potential confusion or ambiguity. Some modern scores use slashes and triangles to show groupings of two and three. Look ahead to exercises 21.17 and 21.18 for other examples.

19.18 ***Toujours léger***

19.19 This excerpt is from the writing of Galileo Galilei (1564 – 1642). What is the language about which he writes? Mathematics. After you have mastered the rhythm, try performing it in canon at an interval of 4 eight notes.

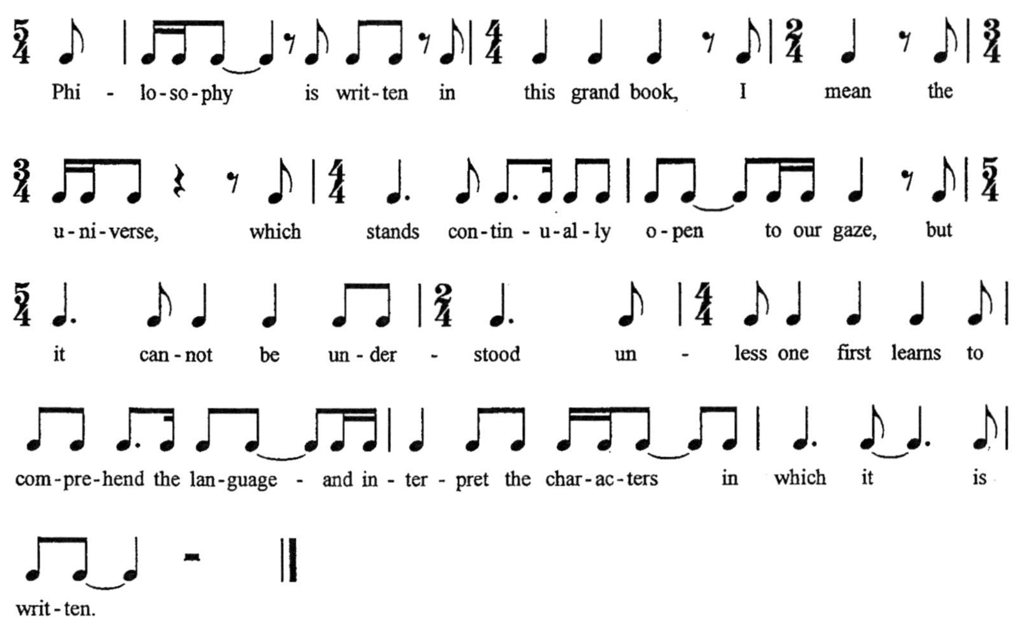

19.20 Twelve-eight is usually a regular compound meter, but not here. Perform this as a speak and clap, duet or with percussion instruments.

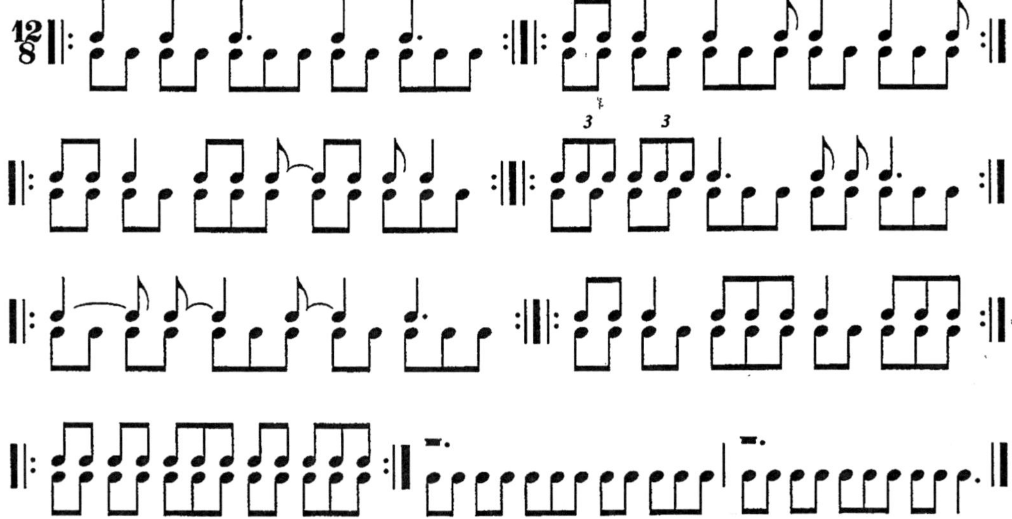

20 ✧ Complex issues in rhythm and meter

Because composers continue to explore new rhythmic relationships and find new ways to notate rhythm, no book on rhythm can ever be complete. This chapter will focus primarily on three areas of innovation: polymeter and cross-rhythm, non-metric rhythm, and unusual supertuplets. Once you have solved these rhythmic challenges, you should have the tools and the experience to tackle other complex rhythm. Exercises in this chapter may require more study and practice than earlier chapters—even rehearsal—but the rewards are well worth the effort.

Polymeter refers to the simultaneous use of two or more meters. **Cross-rhythm** may be used as a synonym for polymeter, or may be used to describe rhythms that imply conflicting meter, but are less regular than polymeter. There are a number of ways to create and notate polymeter or cross-rhythms. Study each example. How are metric accents created? What is the relationship between the meters?

20.1 Perform each line with the correct syllables based on the meter signature. Listen for ways in which meters interact.

Rewrite the first two measures with both parts in 6/8. There are at least two correct ways to notate *ta-di.*

20.2 Meter in the top voice changes when the accents change the grouping. In this case both parts seem to be written in 4/4, but even that is misleading.

20.3 Perform this example both as a speak and clap and as a two-part exercise. Notice that the top line produces four even pulses over five beats. How could the two parts be rewritten?

20.4 Each voice in this example is written with an appropriate meter signature and bar lines. The result is difficult to read in score, and nearly impossible to conduct, but clear to the performers of each line.

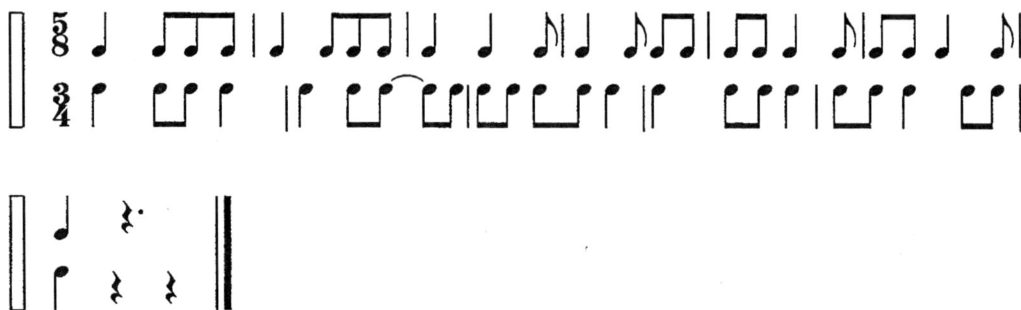

20.5 Although both parts are written in 12/8, the accent patterns suggest changing metric relationships and the eventual creation of cross-rhythms.

20.6 Accent the beginning of each group. Try clapping on each accented note. You may also perform it clapping *just* the accented notes (no speaking).

With vigor!

20.7

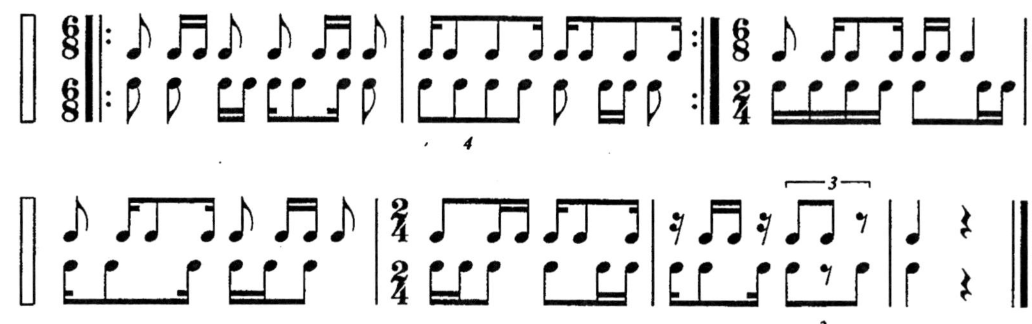

The meters in the next two exercises have an interesting relationship. They share the same number of subdivisions in a measure. The downbeats coincide, but the metric accents within the measure do not.

20.8

20.9

20.10 Decide in advance how many times you will repeat each section, or appoint a leader who will indicate when to move on.

Non-metric rhythm: Music can have a defined rhythm but not be metric. In other words the durations of the individual notes are well defined, but there is no pattern or even sense of accented groupings. The French composer Olivier Messiaen (1908 – 1992) often wrote melodies in this style. Perform this example in a way that highlights the free flowing rhythm. You may have to be creative in assigning syllables.

20.11 *Legato e calmo*

20.12 Unusual groupings make this example a challenge. Rewrite any measures where the groupings are unclear. Why might a composer chose to write it one way or the other?

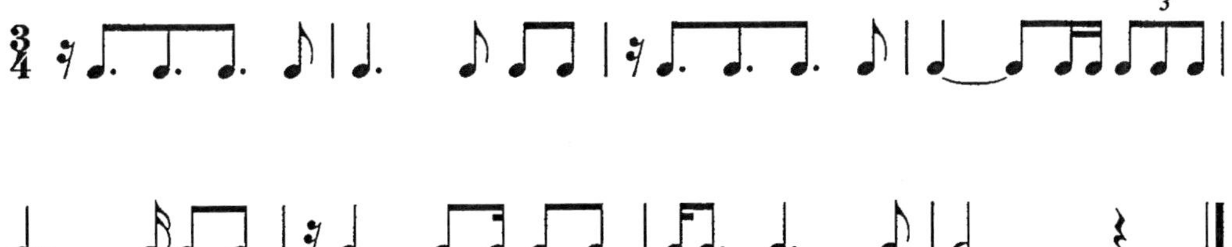

20.13

20.14 Unusual groupings and beat divisions work against the aural perception of regular meter. Perform the example expressively, but focusing on the patterns rather than the notated meter.

En allant et trés espressif

In Chapter 15 we studied supertuplets, and in Chapter 16 we learned about divisions of the beat into five and seven. This chapter explores those irregular divisions spread over more than one beat.

20.15 The quintuplet in this exercise is over two beats. Grouping by two and three may help you keep the durations even (*ta-di ta-ki-da*, for example).

20.16

20.17 In this example the quintuplet fills the measure. You may say *ta* for each note, or group them by two or three (*ta-di ta-ki-da*, for example). Listen to make sure the quintuplet is evenly spaced; and listen also for the unique interaction it creates with the four beats. Do this exercise as a speak and clap or duet, speaking or clapping the parts.

20.18 Practice this exercise speaking and clapping and as a duet until you are able to divide the measure evenly into 5. Listen for the interaction between parts.

20.19

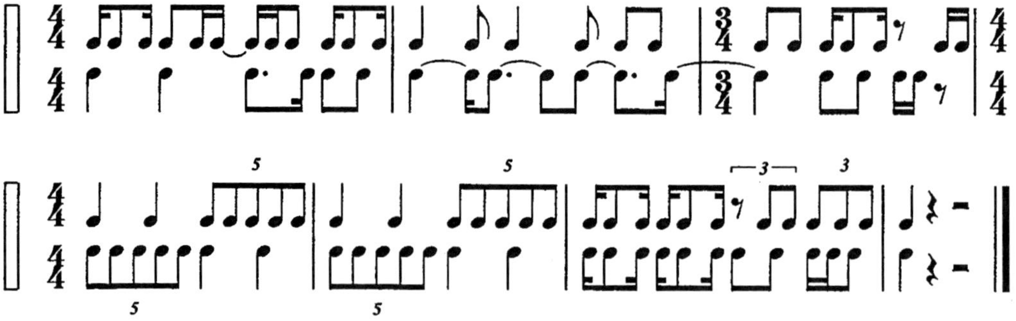

20.20

20.21

21 ✧ Rhythm and meter — Early music and modern music

With the exception of exercises in Chapter 20, most of the rhythm studied so far has been based on music from between about 1600 and 1900, an era when major/minor tonality was at its most influential. Rhythm in music before 1600 and after 1900 was often quite different. This chapter will explore several specific examples of rhythm in both early and more recent musics. There is too much variety to consider every unique rhythmic or metric device, but this sampler will give you a taste of the fascinating variety that is present.

Music from before 1600 often used very complex metric relationships. Take time to understand the notation and plan your approach. Use syllables when they are helpful. Compare and contrast rhythm and meter in this music to what came later. What is similar? What has changed?

21.1 This excerpt based on music from the sixteenth century, mixes simple and compound divisions in some interesting ways.

21.2 This exercise is based on an anonymous French Chace written around 1350. A suggestion for the triplets is given in the first measure.

ta ki di ma

21.3 The short bar lines in this instrumental piece from around 1470 remind us that the music was written without measures and without strong metric accents. Use the groupings and the melodic construction to help you understand the rhythm.

21.4 This exercise is based on music written in about 1470 by Burgundian composer Antoine Busnoys. The meter signature and bar lines help us keep our place, but provide little help in understanding the rhythm organization of the piece. Study the groupings, then listen for the interactions produced by the cross-rhythms.

21.5 The following excerpt is from a motet written around 1290 by Petrus de Cruse. Petrus was among the first composers to divide longer note values into unusual divisions like five and seven.

21.6 This example is based on an excerpt from a motet by the Flemish composer Guillaume Du Fay. It was probably composed around 1460. The bar lines don't go all the way through the staves. Music in the 15th century was written without bar lines and without the same sense of metric accent we have today. Using these short lines call *Mensurstrich* (German for measure line) helps avoid the modern idea of metric accent while still giving the performers something to help them keep their place. Notice too that note values sometimes carry over into the following measure. This happens in the very first measure, for example. Rather than write a tied note over the bar line, the dotted quarter note simply carries over into the beginning of the following measure. This may be difficult to read at first, but it is truer to the original notation.

Music since 1900 has undergone tremendous change, and techniques of rhythm and meter have changed as well. This section will describe and give you a chance to practice a few of the innovative techniques developed in the last 100 years or so. Relate what you find here with music from earlier times.

Elliot Carter (b. 1908) developed the concept of *metric modulation*, a process of changing meter similar in concept to the process of changing keys. Study the next five exercises carefully. How does the meter change? How do these technique differ from those studied in earlier chapters?

21.7 Repeat each measure until you are comfortable with the accent pattern. As the meter "modulates," the accented notes in m. 2 become the beat notes in m. 3. In the next line the meter modulates back to the original 3/4.

21.8

21.9

21.10 The terms metric modulation and *tempo modulation* are related and sometimes used interchangeably. Although the meter doesn't actually change in this example, the tempo changes by a fixed, proportional amount. Study the notation and practice the change in tempo before you perform the excerpt.

21.11 Study the relationship between meters and tempos. How will an eighth note in the final measures compare in length to an eighth note at the beginning?

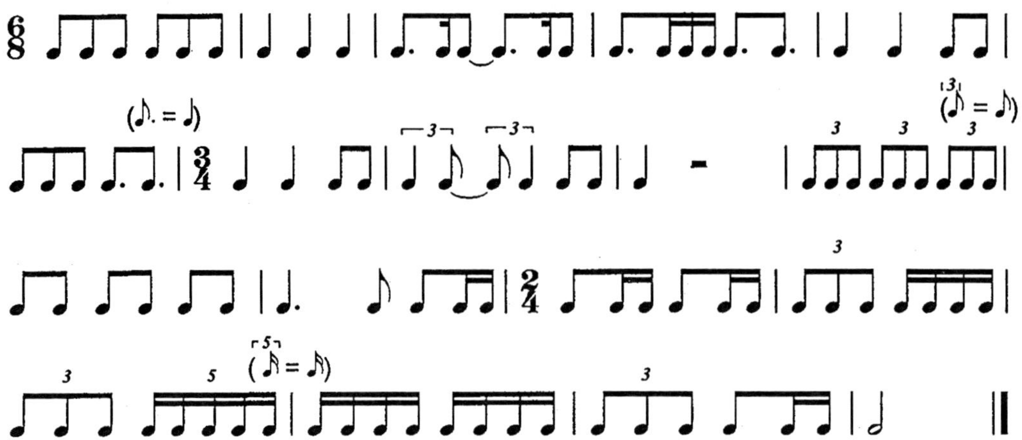

21.12 This exercise shows a type of polymeter associated with the Russian composer Igor Stravinsky (1882 – 1971). The notation of the lower voice suggests a constant 2/4 meter for that part even though it is written with meter changes like the upper voice. Perform it both ways.

21.13 The following exercise based on an excerpt from a choral work by American composer Charles Ives (1874 – 1954) uses changing meter and syncopation to mask any sense of regular metric groupings. Practice it carefully until you can perform it expressively.

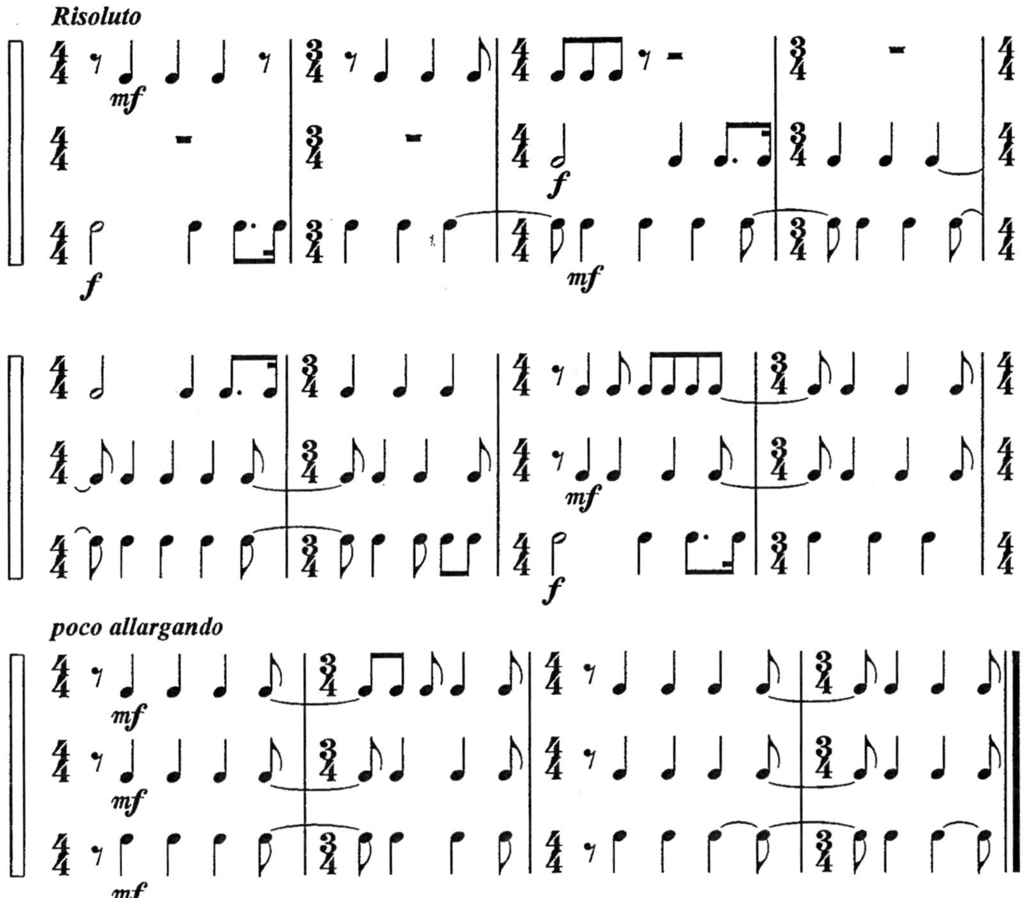

The next three exercises have off-beat and syncopated rhythms characteristic of jazz styles developed in the United States in the early twentieth century. Jazz rhythms are not always notated exactly as written, but sometimes "swing." Your instructor may ask you to perform these rhythms as written, then in a more idiomatic jazz style.

21.14 ***Driving ahead***

21.15 ***In the style of a ballad***

21.16

21.17 This exercise uses rhythms similar to a style made popular by American composer Steve Reich (b. 1936). Composers and conductors often use slashes and triangles above the line to show groupings of two and three. The first two lines have been marked for you. Continue with the third line. Are any measures ambiguous? Make a decision based on context.

21.18 Write in the slashes and triangles for the last two lines.

21.19 Repeat Part I several times, then add Part II. After several repetitions, add Part III. Listen for the interaction of the parts, especially the alignment of rests. This exercise can be clapped, spoken, or played on percussion instruments.

I

II

III

21.20 Begin with Part I; add Part II; then Part III. Or have each performer perform each line as in a canon.

I

II

III

These final two pieces by composer David Madeira (b. 1982) may require a bit more study and practice than some earlier examples, but they will reward the effort.

21.21 Shifting layers of cross-rhythms are a key component of recent innovations in rhythm.

21.22 What is the relationship between the upper and lower parts? Look at the accents if you need a hint. Changing the temporal relationship gradually in this way is sometimes called *phasing*. The parts move out of phase through a complete cycle, then come back into phase by the last repetition. Decide in advance how many times you will repeat each section. Four or five repetitions works well.

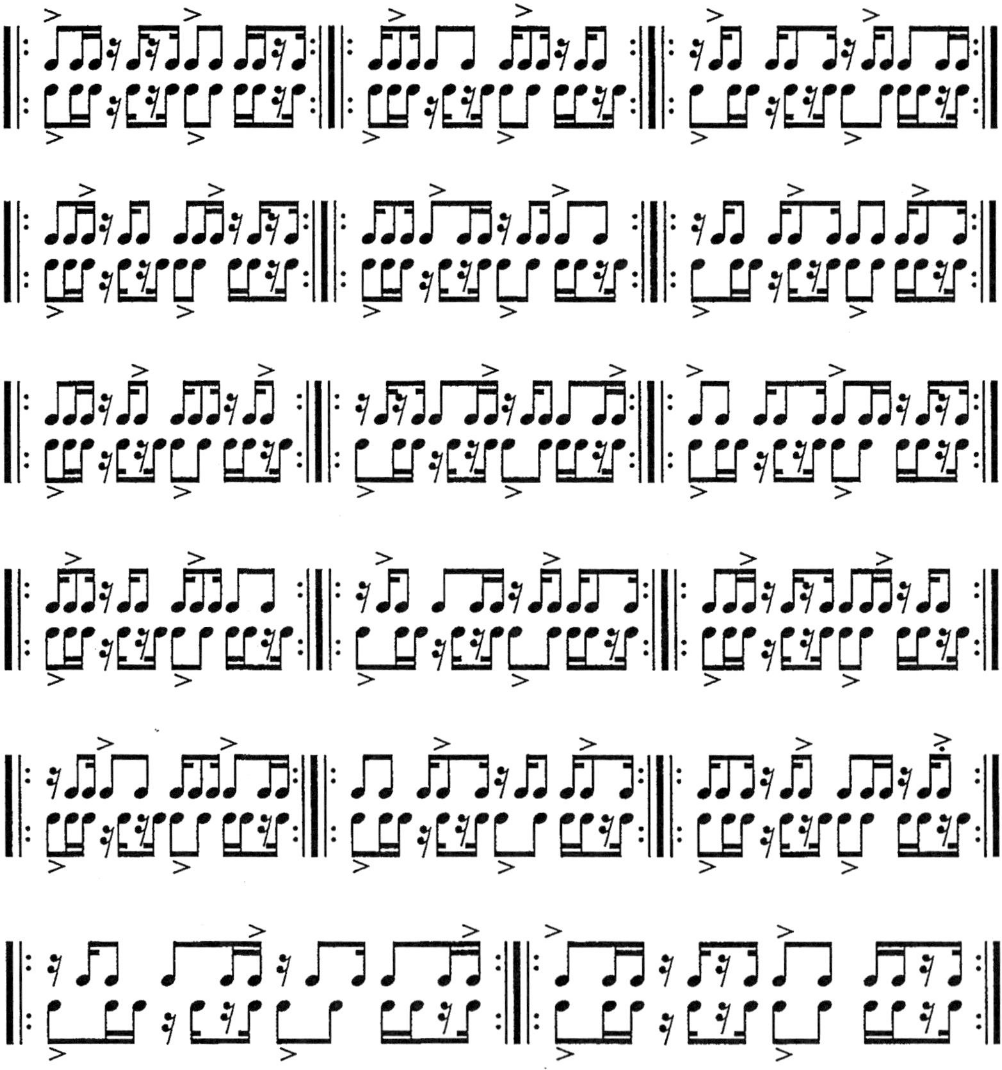

PERFORMANCE TERMS

Foreign terms are frequently used in music to indicate tempo, dynamics, and style. Though the meaning is not always precise, the definitions below are commonly accepted.

A la, Alla (It.): in the style of

A piacere (It.): freely, as you wish

A tempo (It.): at the original tempo (speed)

Accelerando, accel. (It.): gradually becoming faster

Adagio (It.): slow

Allargando (It.): becoming slower, (may imply louder)

Allegro (It.): fast

Allegretto (It.): (. . . *etto* suffix, lit. a little) moderately fast, slower than allegro

Andante (It.): moderate tempo, walking pace

Andantino (It.): may be either somewhat faster or slower than andante, modern usage is faster

Animato (It.): animated, spirited, with life

Assai (It.): very, much

Attacca (It.): begin without a pause

Avec (Fr.): with

Ben (It.): much

Bewegt (Gr.): with movement, agitated

Brio (It.): spirit, vigor

Calando (It.): gradually softer and slower

Cantabile (It.): in a singing style

Cédez (Fr.): gradually slowing

Con (It.): with

Crescendo (It.): becoming louder

Da capo (D.C.) (It.): repeat from the beginning

Dal signo (D.S.) (It.): repeat from the sign (𝄋)

Dolce (It.): sweetly (softly)

Doux (Fr.): sweetly

E, Ed, Et: and

Einfach (Gr.): simple

Empfindung (Gr.): expression

En allant (Fr.): with movement

En dehors (Fr.): prominently, brought out

Etwas (Gr.): somewhat

Fine (It.): the end

Forte (It.): loud

Forza (It.): force, strength

Fröhlich (Gr.): happy, joyful

Fuoco (It.): fire

Geschwind (Gr.): quick

Giusto (It.): exact, steady

Grave (It.): very slow, solemn

Grazioso (It.): graceful

Immer (Gr.): always

Innig (Gr.): with feeling, heartfelt

Kraft (Gr.): strength, power

Kurz (Gr.): short

Langsam (Gr.): slow

Larghetto (It.): somewhat slow

Largo (It.): slow (may imply broad)

Lebhaft (Gr.): lively

Legato (It.): smooth and connected

Léger (Fr.): light

Leggero (It.): light delicate

Leise (Gr.): lightly

Lent (Fr.): slow

Lento (It.): slow

Ma (It.): but

Maestoso (It.): majestic, dignified

Marcato (It.): marked, accented

Mässig (Gr.): moderate

Meno (It.): less

Mesto (It.): sad

Mit (Gr.): with

Mezzo (It.): lit. half or middle; moderately

Molto (It.): much, very

Möglich (Gr.): possible

Morendo (It.): dying away

Mosso (moto) (It.): motion, movement

Nicht (Gr.): not

Niente (It): nothing

Non (It.): not

Perdendosi (It.): dying (fading) away

Pesante (It.): heavy, ponderous

Piacevole (It.): pleasant, agreeable

Piano (It.): soft

Pianissimo (It.): (. . . issimo suffix lit. very) very soft

Più (It.): more

Poco (It.): a little

Presto (It.): very fast

Rallentando (It.): gradually becoming slower, implies broader

Rasch (Gr.): fast

Ritardando, Rit. (It.): gradually becoming slower

Rubato (It.): lit. stolen; indictes freedom and flexibility of tempo

Ruhig (Gr.): peaceful

Scherzando (It.): playful, lively

Schnell (Gr.): fast

Sehr (Gr.): very

Sempre (It.): always, continuously

Senza (It.): without

Simile (It.): similarly, in the same manner

Sostenuto (It.): sustained

Sotto voce (It.): softly, with a subdued voice

Staccato (It.): detached

Stark (Gr.): strong, vigorous

Stringendo (It.): gradually faster

Subito (It.): suddenly

Teneramente (It.): tenderly

Tenuto (It.): sustained, held

Toujours (Fr.): always

Trés (Fr.): very

Triste (Fr.): sadly

Troppo (It.): much

Un peu (Fr.): a little

Und (Gr.): and

Wie (Gr.): as

Vif (Fr.): lively

Vivace (It.): quick, lively

Zart (Gr.): tender, soft

Ziemlich (Gr.): somewhat, rather